Yet More

TYBEE ISLAND

HEROES AND HOOLIGANS

The Making of an Island Paradise, Vol. 3

I0778342

J.R. ROSEBERRY

Cover Art: The photograph features this book's author seated in front of Tybee Island's iconic lighthouse. It was taken by popular Tybee writer and photographer Ben Goggins, while the cover itself was created by layout designer Lauren Clackum. The caricatures surrounding the photo, each of which was drawn by Mallory Pearce, represent the characters featured in this book.

Paperback ISBN: 978-1-959563-21-1
Hardback ISBN: 978-1-959563-22-8
eBook ISBN: 978-1-959563-23-5

Published by:
Maudlin Pond Press
P.O. Box 53
Tybee Island, GA 31328
www.maudlinpond.com

Dedicated to
Carla Donen Davis

Seventy years of loving memories and....

...occasional thoughts of what might have been.

Preface

This book is the third volume of my series.

In it you will find 24 new characters whose lives are part of the larger life and magic of Tybee Island. Read on and I hope you will catch my drift.

Small towns are special places.

I've lived in my share of them – places like Leonardtown and LaPlata, Maryland and a small village outside Naha, Okinawa.

Such places are small enough to enable residents to develop a sense of community and camaraderie which was absent in the big cities where I lived.

Tybee Island, a small town situated beside the sea – or at the edge of the earth as some like to say – is extra special.

Its residents have created a community of folks who not only welcome, but actually care about one another. Islanders represent a potpourri of people with dramatically different beliefs and backgrounds who congregate comfortably under one enormous, open-minded beach umbrella.

Where else can you find annual events like a Beach Bum Parade (the longest rolling water fight in the world!), a Juneteenth celebration, Martin Luther King Jr. Parade, an ocean Polar Bear Plunge, and a Pirates' Festival, in addition to active music, dance, art, theatrical and civic groups along with an abundance of wildlife, a pristine beach, and ocean and river recreation?

It's the people, of course, that make Tybee so special. I want to give a special thanks to those who read the first volume in this series, and hence are familiar with my own discovery of the island. A reprint of that introduction is provided below for new readers.

I was in my early 20s when Tybee seduced me.

Situated just down the road from Savannah, more than a few things about the island turned my head.

Her beauty was ubiquitous, from her willowy, windswept dunes to her miles of pristine beach bordering, depending on her mood, either crashing or calmly serene surf, it was a photographer's paradise.

It was paradise in other ways as well for an energetic young reporter for the Savannah Morning News.

Populated by eccentric, hard-drinking party-lovers, its raucous bars made Tybee the polar opposite of what was then Savannah's sleepy ambience.

Preachers and politicians, scions of society and scallywags, lawyers, gamblers, fishermen, musicians, and artists rubbed shoulders on its beaches and in its bistros.

I fell in love with the island, deeply and permanently.

The job at the Savannah newspaper was my first since leaving Tokyo, where from 1957 to 1960 I had pursued post graduate studies in philosophy while working for Pacific Stars & Stripes, the Associated Press and the Okinawa Morning Star.

My shift at the newspaper, covering city hall before being named editor of Savannah Magazine, was from 3 p.m. to 11 p.m. or so, depending on the events of the day.

When my workday ended, there was little happening in Savannah, where only one bar, the Port Royal, was then operating on River Street.

In contrast, Tybee's bars were alive and filled with music-loving, beer-guzzling locals who were quick to befriend anyone on an adjacent bar stool at face value, rarely asking where they were from or what they did for a living.

After hoisting a few, the natives often regaled you with tales of Tybee's past, some of which had an ominous edge.

Semi-inebriated islanders said there had been no rapes or murders on Tybee for years because most miscreants knew how locals dealt with such felonies.

Their stories described how they'd drag malevolent offenders aboard a shrimp boat and drop them off the stern when the shrimpers lowered their nets while heading out to sea.

For lesser offenses like robberies or break-ins, culprits might be hauled over to Little Tybee, buried up to their chests in the sand, have honey poured on their heads, and be left to try to extricate themselves before ants and gulls had a picnic.

I never knew whether the tales were true or simply cautionary warnings, but, like others who heard them, I was not inclined to find out.

With no mandated closing time, Tybee's beach-side bacchanal often lasted till dawn, providing stress relief and a plethora of new pleasures enlivening my existence and expanding my horizons.

More often than many mature folks might find reasonable, I found myself driving back to Savannah with eyes watering from the burning sunrise reflected in the rear-view mirror.

Those were the "good old days" I found on Tybee 62 years ago, before heading north to continue my newspaper career with the Norfolk Virginian-Pilot from

1962 to 1967 and the Washington Post from 1967 to 1992.

Based on that early exposure to Tybee, when it came time to retire from the Post, I headed back to the island, looking for the good vibes I remembered to help me decide what I wanted to do with the rest of my life and where I wanted to do it.

My plan was to hunker down near the beach for a month to get my head around such stuff. That was 30 years ago, and I never left.

Once I realized I was here to stay, I expanded my interests well beyond those initial bar-hopping days.

I joined the "Y" and helped start a senior's club there; joined four friends in initiating the annual New Year's Day Polar Bear Plunge which now draws thousands; promoted the first official and now annual New Year's Eve celebration on the South End; helped salvage the old Post Theater when it was about to be demolished; and helped create a DeSoto Beach Hotel exhibit in the Lighthouse Museum to preserve memories of the island's storied old Mediterranean-style hotel.

Along the way I met dozens of islanders who had lived and were still living extraordinary lives and became convinced that their stories should be shared before they were lost forever.

Bitten once again
by the writing bug, I
started a weekly col-
umn in what was then
the Savannah newspa-
per's "Closeup" section
called "J.R.'s Island
View." The column
introduced readers to
often little-known but
fascinating folks who
lived on or near Tybee
Island.

Early (circa 1997) fan Mary Slater enjoys Closeup column with morning smoke and coffee.

The columns not only described their impressive accomplishments but told of their escapades and foi-
bles. Based on the positive feedback from readers, the
column succeeded in providing its audience with a bit
of informative and refreshing reading over morning
coffee.

Since becoming somewhat more reflective as I've
grown considerably longer in the tooth, it occurred to
me that those stories, collectively, captured a snap-
shot of what Tybee was like a quarter century ago.

Many long-time Tybee residents now believe those
were the "real" good old days.

This book is a compilation of some those old columns
and photos.

They've been assembled in the hope that they may help those who were here at the time savor some pleasant memories and may provide newcomers with a slice of easy-to-swallow island history.

For recent island arrivals, I suspect today will become their own good old days when they think about them 25 years from now, years that will pass far faster than most can imagine.

With luck, the current crop of writers will help them enjoy these treasured memories one day, just as I'm hoping to do with this book.

POSTSCRIPT: You will see postscripts after most chapters to let you know what has happened to the folks I've written about since I first put their stories to paper.

Some have passed away or moved away, and some have vanished without a trace (that is, without giving me a chance to put them into my witness protection).

If you have information that I do not, please send it my way to P.O. Box 1503, Tybee Island, GA 31328 or jayrose@juno.com.

Table of Contents

Benjamin Alexander -
Recalling the Island's Glory Days

Entrepreneur
Brought Music
To the Beach

*H*e remembers the glory days of entertainment on Tybee and in Savannah.

Benjamin J. "Bennie" Alexander was a major force in the business around these parts in the beginning, back in the 1930s.

Bennie, now 87, brought in the first big name bands, drawing huge crowds to the old Tybee pavilion, and he's still got some ideas about how to generate business on the new one.

When he first came to the island, Highway 80 was a dirt road from Thunderbolt out to the beach.

"Hell, people never even heard of Tybee back then, but they damned well knew who Ted Weems was," says Bennie, discussing the former popular band leader who became his biggest draw.

"The crowds were backed up in line all the way to

Butler Ave. and around the corner to attend the
Weems performance," says Bennie. "They stood in
two lines, one down Strand and the other up 16th and
around Butler back to where Cap'n Chris' is now."

Bennie arrived on the island in 1936 serving as business
manager for Henry Digini and his Casiloma
Band, a group he had been with for almost ten years.
He joined them in Youngstown, Ohio where he was
working in a steel mill.

Bennie Alexander 1937.

His mother had a large house in Youngstown, and the band played at Isiah Park, a half mile away, every summer. While there, the band booked room and board at his mother's house.

Bennie took to attending the group's performances and eventually was asked if he wanted to join them as a driver while learning the booking business on road trips.

"I said, hell, I'm just making $1.50 a day in the steel mill, of course I want to join you!"

Bennie hit the road with the band which toured the entire country on one-night stands. That was the start of his life-long career in show business.

He was the group's manager by the time they signed up for their first Tybee engagement, and after beach appearances the next two years, he decided to linger on the laid-back little island.

That was 60 years ago and Bennie's still here.

His younger brother, Nickie Alexander, has been a mainstay of Tybee's business community for years.

Nickie still operates a bail bonding business near the corner of Tybrisa and Butler, where both brothers operated bars for almost 50 years.

Bennie became ill in the summer of 1939 and had to leave Digini's band to return to Ohio for an operation.

Tommy McCarroll, a friend he met on Tybee, drove to Ohio to bring him back after the operation and put him up in his own island house.

McCarroll, who owned the Novelty Bar, trusted Bennie so much he hired him as his bar manager and put the place in Bennie's name.

Later, Willie Haar, owner of the old Rip Tide Bar, talked Bennie into taking over that bar as well, in addition to handling bookings on the old pavilion, which Haar also owned.

"Willie gave me the bar, a bowling alley and a hot dog stand on the pavilion, all for $3,500 a year," says Bennie. "We split the take on the pavilion."

"I stayed at the old Tybee Hotel on the ocean front. It was real nice. I don't know why the hell they ever tore that place down. It was nicer than anything down here since."

That was in the early 1940s when Bennie says his pavilion bookings started drawing "the biggest crowds they ever had."

His biggest coup was hiring the Ted Weems orchestra for a one-night stand.

"I stole Ted Weems," says Bennie, grinning. "I got him for $1,000."

He also brought in Cab Calloway, Tommy Tucker, and other big bands.

4

After his success on Tybee, Bennie headed for Savannah in the mid-1940s to take over Al Remler's famous Club Royale at the corner of Victory Drive and Skidaway.

He hired his brother Nickie, who had just been discharged from the Army, to run the Rip Tide. Nickie later operated a liquor store and several clubs on the island's south end.

Bennie looked dapper in the 1940s.

"Nickie's done real good," says Bennie. "I'm happy for him. He's done better than I did. He's used his head."

"The Club Royale was 20 years ahead of its time," claims Bennie. "The bar alone seated 125 and we could get 500 people in the dining room. It cost maybe a million dollars to build that place."

He and a partner, Jimmy Brown, leased the club for $800 a month.

"I was doing so damned much business that they stationed federal boys at the gate to check the crowds, counting every person, to make sure the place didn't become an overcrowded fire trap," recalls Bennie.

He says his best night at the club came "when I hired Vincent Lopez for $500," when his regular fees were far higher, because Lopez had a free traveling night and called Bennie to find out if he had an opening in the area.

"He said he'd take anything," recalls Bennie. "He just wanted to play somewhere. I stole him. We took in $5,000 that night."

"I gave Guy Lombardo $3,500 for one night. I gave Harry James, Tommy Dorsey, and Jimmy Dorsey $2,500 each for a night. Harry James brought his wife, Betty Grable, along with him. I think Xavier Cugat was the last band I had in there."

The Club Royale had over 150 slot machines ,and

they were making big money at the time. The C&S
Bank, which financed construction of the huge club,
got its money back from the slot machine revenue
alone, according to Bennie.

"What they didn't know was that each of the old machines had a coin tube that held $20 or more, and you
could press a button and clear the tube. The C&S had
the keys to the machines and collected that money,
but Remler was clearing the tubes. He got his off the
top," laughs Bennie.

The club closed not long after authorities shut down
the slot machine operation. It was later torn down to
construct a shopping center.

Bennie says before they were outlawed, slot machines
were a main source of revenue for businesses in both
Savannah and Tybee.

"Heck, I remember when old man Chu (founder
of Chu's Department Store and the Chu dynasty
throughout the area) first started with a little stand
at the beach on Strand. He had two slot machines on
his counter. He started with that, and he wound up
owning almost the entire island."

Bennie bailed out of the Club Royale when he learned
that despite his entertainment success on weekends,
he was unable to make enough during the week to
cover the overhead.

"It was just too expensive to operate," he says. "We
had over a hundred waitresses and five bartenders.

It just cost too much. The timing was wrong, and you couldn't compete with Johnny Harris down the street. He was an institution."

Bennie says a friend came to his rescue when he asked him to run another bar, the Sportsman's Club, in Garden City.

"He told me I was paying $800 rent for the Club Royale, and he'd let me have his place, including an apartment and six cabins out back, for $275."

"I did real good there too. I had close ties to the authorities, and they let me stay open until five in the morning. I was packing them in."

But he ran into trouble when a buddy started bringing his young girlfriend to the bar.

"I kept telling him don't bring that girl in here," says Bennie. "She's only 17 and you're gonna get me in trouble. Don't bring her in here no more. Stay the hell out of here!"

Bennie beside oversized convertible in 1941.

Shortly after issuing this edict Benny found himself in bigger trouble than he had imagined.

His friend had an argument with the girl and took her to the parking lot out back where he shot and killed her with a gun he stole from Bennie's office.

Authorities closed the club down for two months and "it cost me 20 grand to get my license back," he says.

Bennie reopened the bar, renaming it the Stork Club, and business started booming again, but once again was short lived.

He ran into a tax problem and was shut down after a competitor "ratted on me," he says. "That S.O.B. wasn't doing any business himself and couldn't stand seeing the crowds at my place."

That experience soured Bennie on area club operations, so he took a break from the local scene to head for California.

Virtually broke, he rented a small apartment not far from the Los Angeles airport and walked from there to a car lot just down the street to ask for work.

"I told 'em I'd never sold a car before, and they said you're just the kind of person we're looking for. I sold a car my first day on the job and by the second year I was their top salesman. They made me the sales manager after that."

Bennie had been on the West Coast about five years

when he got a call from Emory Bobo who was purchasing most of Willie Haar's extensive business
holdings on Tybee's south end.

"Bobo asked me to take over the Brass Rail down by
the beach. I told him I was happy where I was, that I
was doing real good, but he said he really wanted me.
I agreed to take it if he'd let me buy the place from
him for $40,000."

Bennie said the bar, which had a big back room on
the end facing the ocean, was doing very little business at the time and he was amazed when crowds
showed up from the first day he took over the operation.

"I never had a bad night," he says. "I had a 14-piece
band, Joe Logano, with a drummer who really put on
a show. He'd do a solo that lasted forever, and I got a
couple of pretty girls to go up there in the middle of
it and spray him down with water bottles."

"The crowd went crazy over that. They were standing
in line to get in the place."

Bennie also hired four go-go girls and two strippers,
and he conducted a little gaming operation back of
the bar.

"We were raking in the money," he recalls, noting
that crowds came from Savannah and Ft. Screven, an
active army base at the time, and soldiers flocked to
the beach bars which stayed open all night.

The local constabulary rarely bothered the bar operations, according to Bennie.

Occasionally, however, word would come that state or federal authorities were headed toward the island to crack down on shady operations.

When that happened, insiders would make a quick phone call to the bridge tender at the old Bull River drawbridge which had to be cranked open and closed by hand, a process that could take more than an hour.

After being alerted, the bridge tender would crank the bridge open, blocking authorities from proceeding to the island long enough to give the bar owners time to close or shut down their questionable activities.

Bennie says just when he was hitting his peak at the Brass Rail, the owners foreclosed on Bobo's mortgage before he could raise the money to buy the place.

"They locked me out," he says. "Padlocked the place! They shouldn't have done that. They got greedy when they saw those crowds I was drawing. They wanted to take the place over."

But Bennie had the last laugh by proving that it was not the bar but his entrepreneurship that made it a success.

He claims the new operator "went busted within two months" when the crowds evaporated.

The good times were changing in other areas at the beach as well.

The glory days pretty much disappeared after a killer storm wrecked the old pavilion and "finally some fool lit a match to it" and burned it down, says Bennie, who headed back to Savannah in 1965 to open the Windjammer on Victory Drive and the Red Light Lounge on 68th and Waters Ave.

"The Lounge was the best club I ever had," he says. "I'd open up at 5 at night and close at 3 in the morning. It was beautiful. I got all the doctors and nurses."

He also opened bars named Bennie I, Bennie II and Bennie III at various locations around Savannah, along with a bar called The Party Lounge at Pennsylvania and President Streets.

"Hell, I had more bars in those days than you could shake a stick at," he smiles.

Bennie operated those bars until 1984, then spent a brief time in the vending machine business before finally retiring when he reached his late 70s.

The only beach buildings remaining from the old days, he says, are the Carbo House and Doc's Bar on Tybrisa, Christy's on Strand and the building which housed the old Red Barn (now Kitten's Korner).

"Tybee's not the same anymore," he laments.

"The problem now is that you've got people here that don't know how to run this damned town. They fight you. Every time you want to do anything they fight it, and there are just too damned many bars down there (at the south end). There's not enough people to keep 'em all in business."

But the venerable octogenarian's eyes still light up when he talks about the new pavilion.

"That pavilion could be packed every night," he says. "You could put a local band up there and draw crowds. Entertainment! That's the only thing that's going to draw people. Fix it up where you can dance!"

"Then you could take that part of the floor off and put a roller-skating floor down when there's no band. That's what we did. That old pavilion was never empty."

Bennie, left, with friend on West Bay Street in1993.

"And they ought to be getting big name entertainment on the pavilion. It's a natural. Hell, I've still got connections all over. I could book in some big names right now!"

Based on his experience, and the renewed vigor he displays when speculating on such stuff, you figure it's a safe bet that he could.

POSTSCRIPT: Several big bands have been hired to perform on the pavilion on special occasions recently and, just as he predicted, they drew large crowds, but Bennie was no longer around to enjoy them. He passed away on March 14, 1997, shortly after this was written.

Richard Grosse -

Not a Typical Short Order Cook

Erudite Restaurateur Travelled the World On Missions for U.S.

*H*e's an average looking guy-medium height and weight, gray hair curling beneath the edges of a dingy white cap, its plastic, adjustable straps unhooked and dangling in back-flipping hamburgers and fetching French fries from the deep fat fryer.

A rumpled apron is draped over his trousers and nondescript socks emerge from his stained cloth sneakers as he shuffles from the freezer to the grill to the cash register at the Sugar Shack which squats on a corner beside U.S. 80 on Tybee Island.

The horn-rimmed glasses make him look somewhat studious, but you figure they may be an affectation, something intended to set him apart from your typical Tybee short order cook... maybe even make him seem bookish.

Between orders he leans over the counter where he is, in fact, engrossed in a pair of books. You figure they're probably trivial beach fare and he's likely just skimming one then the other, since you can skip most of the doggerel in this stuff anyway.

Then, when he heads back to grill up another order, you glance at his reading material. It's not the Danielle Steele or Robin Cook you expected.

One is a book of Mozart sheet music, written in Latin. The other's a couple of thousand pages of Francis Parkman's 1875 account of Count Frontenac and New France under Louis XIV, an obscure tome describing the struggle between France and England for dominance in North America.

Richard Grosse is not your typical Tybee grill meister.

Actually, he and Mary, his wife of 42 years, own the Sugar Shack and, while it's often mistaken by vacationers as being just another beach burger and ice cream shop, they offer some rather esoteric fare.

Take the pan-broiled sole fillet, for instance. It's prepared with garlic, scallions and white wine sauce.

Just a little something Richard became enamored of while enroute to France when his plane developed engine trouble and was forced to land in Iceland. After savoring the sole at a Reykjavik restaurant, he cornered the chef to glean the recipe and determine where he obtained the ingredients.

Turns out that everything but the sole itself came from the U.S.

And, while the couple has owned the establishment
for a quarter century, it's certainly not what Richard
is all about.

He's fluent in French, having studied that language in
France prior to entering Yale; conversant in German;
has studied Greek, and obviously has a pretty good
working knowledge of Latin, among other languages.
After graduating from Yale, where he studied history
and diplomacy, he did graduate work in public law
and government at Columbia University, studying
under Zbigniew Brzezinski, who was later National
Security Adviser in the Carter Administration.

Then he entered the foreign service with the State
Department.

Richard's mother, incidentally, was Virginia Shaw,
the first licensed female flight instructor in the United States back in 1935. She was one of the first females to land a plane on
an aircraft carrier, and
during World War II she
instructed navy pilots.

Back in the 1930s she
gained considerable fame
in show business as one
of Gene Kelly's dance
partners and, late in her
life, she served as an instructor at the Gretchin
Green Dance School on
Wilmington Island.

*Richard Grosse dressed for
church at the Sugar Shack.*

Richard's foreign service career was not spent in a humdrum office in Washington, although he did work in that city for a time in U.N. affairs and national security, coordinating activities with the C.I.A. and other agencies.

That was just after his tour in Bonn, Germany during the formative stages of the European Common Market.

"My job was to persuade the Germans to be kind to American agriculture," he says. "I think I persuaded them, but I'm not sure the Germans persuaded the French or some of the others."

His first foreign service posting, in 1955, was to Leopoldville in the Belgian Congo, then referred to as "Darkest Africa."

Richard's specialty was political and economic reporting on French Equatorial Africa, now known as Gabon, which at the time was a huge, thinly populated swarth of that continent.

"Mary and I were the first married couple ever sent to that post," he says.

Richard became one of the honored few to have a passing acquaintance with Dr. Albert Schweitzer while on this assignment.

His contact with the Nobel Prize winning doctor came in 1956, when he was called upon to lead literary lion Norman Cousins and a group of doctors to

Schweitzer's remote compound in Lambarene.

Cousins, editor of the Saturday Review, noted author
and adviser to presidents, was a Schweitzer enthusiast and wanted to witness the doctor's work before
arranging funding for a modern medical facility in
that location.

Because he was fluent in German and French, the latter being the language in which Schweitzer conversed,
Richard was assigned to meet the entourage at the
airport in Libreville, lead the expedition to Lambarene, and serve as interpreter.

"I had to cross the Congo River at Brazzaville to
reach Leopoldville and catch a plane to Libreville,
then take the group on a river boat up to Lambarene," he recalls.

"There were enormous mahogany trees leaning out
over the twisting river. The darkness and the light
coming through these trees was like a scene from Con-
rad's *Heart of Darkness*. It was an incredible scene,
and with the immense heat there at the equator it
was breathtaking."

Once the initial meetings were held, Richard was able
to spend some time alone with the doctor discussing
the encroachment of "civilization" on developing
countries.

"Dr. Schweitzer was not enthusiastic about efforts
to modernize his hospital at the time," says Richard.
"He liked the village community type of hospital. He

said you can't tear a culture out of a people by the roots.

"The natives just wandered in and out of his hospital. It was like a village. People were cooking and eating right there in the hospital. And there was no air conditioning. It was open to the air. But it was ideal for the Africans at that time, and he was doing marvelous things with tropical diseases."

Richard and the doctor discussed the inevitable advance of technology in the area as natives learned of modern conveniences and developed a desire for them.

He says he told the doctor that, whether it was good or bad, "we were going to have to live through the transition."

"Schweitzer said 'You're going to have to live through it. I'm not!'"

Richard's fondest recollection of his time with the doctor was spending a late evening with him at his house as Schweitzer played Bach's Toccata and Fugue in E Minor on an old pump organ.

"That was something to hear in the middle of Africa. He was a marvelous organist, and at his age, well into his 80s, a marvelous interpreter of Bach."

Richard knows a little something about music.

He once sang with the Yale Glee Club and has sung in church choirs for 50 years.

*Richard and omni-present pipe takes a break with Mary
at their restaurant.*

And that Mozart sheet music he was perusing at his restaurant? He's using it to prepare for a performance with the Savannah Symphony Orchestra.

Richard sings bass with the orchestra, performing in a number of the group's presentations each year.

Among the other highlights of his tour in Africa were occasional excursions into the bush with Mary.

On one of these he shot and wounded a water buffalo "and a wounded water buffalo is kind of dangerous," says Richard, who tends to be a bit understated.

"We had Mary, who was three months pregnant at the time, climb up a tree for safety while I joined the others in hiking through the underbrush, trying to locate the animal before someone was hurt.

"I fell into a sink hole while we were searching and disappeared. The thing was about nine feet deep, and I had the only rifle in the group," he laughs.

Eventually, he and his rifle were extricated, and the group finally found the animal after hiking for about 18 miles through rough terrain.

On another occasion Richard was placed in charge of logistics for the initial phase of a high-profile safari.

TV personality Arthur Godfrey and Gen. Curtis Lemay, then head of the U.S. Strategic Air Command, flew into Chad for an elephant hunt in the Fort Archambeault region of the middle Congo.
"They were both kind of flamboyant personalities, and the Belgian ambassador called to make sure they were treated right and didn't go hog wild," says Richard, who was assigned to get them from Chad to Fort Archambeault for the safari.

"They landed there with a whole plane full, a mountain of stuff they brought for the hunt," he says.

"I asked them how they expected to get all their stuff to Fort Archambeault, and they said they'd just charter a bus and drive over.

"The roads and trails were so bad you'd have a hard

time getting through with a Jeep," he laughs. "Driving a bus would have been impossible!"

Richard finally got the two famous men to winnow their paraphernalia somewhat and crammed them and their remaining cargo into a Jeep for the harrowing 380-mile drive to Fort Archambeault, from where they headed out for their hunt.

After his Washington assignment, Richard says he left the foreign service "because it was just too cumbersome to ferry four children around the world" and he and Mary now had four sons.

Then he took a break to obtain his MBA degree from New York University's graduate school of business "so I could apply what I learned overseas to the business community."

In 1966 he and Mary and their four sons moved to Tybee when Richard was employed by a company in Savannah, assisting in setting up an exporting business.

"Where else would you want to live?" he says of choosing to reside on Tybee. "It's got an ocean and a beach!"

Richard remained with that company for ten years before starting his own Grosse & Co., exporting heavy machinery and construction equipment.

He sold that company in 1984.

Prior to selling that company, he and Mary purchased the Sugar Shack location in 1971, and Mary was running the operation.

After initially living in a house near the beach on 7th Street, they purchased a large section of the old gun emplacements near the museum at Ft. Screven when it came on the market in 1970.

"I had about 2,000 feet of oceanfront and eight acres of land," he recalls.

They built a huge home at the fort, "with about 11,000 square feet of space," he says. "The inside was modeled after a chalet we'd seen in the Pyrenees."

They even had a swimming pool atop the huge cement gun emplacement overlooking the ocean.

After selling his company, Richard started working with Mary at the Sugar Shack. While this may sound tame after their globe-trotting adventures, Richard says he enjoys the place and there may be more to the restaurant's operation than meets the eye.

"It's permitted us to send our four boys to four different Ivy League colleges," he says, with obvious satisfaction.

Besides, Richard has interests in addition to the shop and the symphony.

He has served in mission work for the Presbyterian Church, travelling extensively through Central America, sitting in on discussions of Christianity versus Marxism.

"I was in Nicaragua during the Sandinista time," he says, noting, "It got interesting, very interesting; kind of like visiting Nazi Germany. Kind of scary."

He also collects primitive African and South American art, specializing in the work of Bantu artisans.

Richard says he was amazed to find a graphic illustration of cultural transference in South America where he discovered "the exact models of chairs made by former slaves in Surinam, thousands of miles away."

Mary Odom Grosse.

Although he no longer works with foreign missions, Richard remains active in Presbyterian Church business.

He's also a published poet and serves on the board and is former president of the Georgia Poetry Society in Savannah.

And Richard has worked for more than 20 years with the Corps of Engineers and Tybee city officials in connection with beach renourishment and determining the causes of erosion among other environmental projects.

Your typical Tybee short order cook, he's not.

POSTSCRIPT: Richard Louis Grosse passed away on June 13, 2007. Mary Odom Grosse, his wife of 52 years, continued operating the Sugar Shack until she retired at age 88. She was well known on Tybee for her fast-paced, six-mile daily walks around the north end of the island which she continued for decades. She gained fame throughout the area when she set the USA Track & Field American Masters 10K record (for women aged 85 to 89) at the 2016 Enmarket Savannah Bridge Run. Mary was 92 when she passed away on July 30, 2023.

Margaret Palmer -
Globe Trotter Achieves Her Goal

Brings World
Of Experience
Back Home

On warm summer nights, she used to lie on Tybee's beach with her dad, looking up at the stars and dreaming about far off lands.

He nurtured those dreams and encouraged her penchant for adventure, taught her about stars and constellations, and would sometimes point toward the moonbeam-streaked surf saying: "Over there is Africa!"

Going there became her goal, but she often wondered if she'd ever have the opportunity.

Margaret Palmer fulfilled that dream and a myriad of others, but not right away.

First, she frolicked through her childhood on Tybee in the early 1900s, fishing and crabbing in the ocean, shrimping in creeks along the Back River, and romping over the dunes with her handful of playmates.

Except for the troops stationed at Fort Screven, she says there were only eight families residing on the island through the winter in those days.

But the warm days of summer were filled with things to do and new friends to do them with as folks from Savannah and more distant places returned to the island.

"We'd wade out in the ocean by the rocks on the north end and just scoop up crabs, there were so many of them," she recalls, "and we never bought seafood. We could catch all we wanted right here."

In addition to the seafood caught locally, a Daufuskie Island resident rowed a boat over to Tybee each day and strolled along the boardwalk selling fresh produce.

Later, when the road to the beach was completed, a Wilmington Island farmer drove out and sold vegetables from his truck. A scale hanging on chains was always swinging at the rear of the vehicle.

"You bought what you needed right away because we had no refrigeration," recalls Margaret.

That was back when island houses had no electricity, the sewer system and even septic tanks had not yet arrived. Pot-bellied stoves were used for cooking and provided what heat was needed.

The glass shades on kerosene lamps utilized for illumination required daily cleaning and that was Margaret's principal assignment and her least favorite chore.

She says she used old newspapers to polish the shades because "there's something in the oil of a newspaper that's wonderful for cleaning glass, but it was a smutty job and I hated cleaning those lamps."

When the septic systems finally arrived, they were a cause for celebration, providing what some might consider unusual fun for Margaret and her playmates.

"They were delivered by train and a number of them were unloaded at each station," she says. "The winter before they were installed, we would play in them for hours, climbing in and out and through the tanks."

"And old Dr. James Nottingham Carter had a pony he would let us ride. There couldn't have been a more wonderful place to grow up!"

Margaret was brought to the island as a tot when her parents moved out from Savannah because her father, Thomas R. Jones, became ill.

Jones, an editorial writer for the Savannah Morning News and head of the city's Chamber of Commerce for many years, suffered from Blackwater Fever, the symptoms of which were similar to a malignant malaria, and a doctor told him Tybee had "a very salubrious climate" which might help him improve.

It turned out that this advice was just what the doctor ordered and "dad's health improved immediately, and my parents fell in love with the island," says Margaret.

The few permanent residents and most vacationers stayed in cottages on the beach side of Butler, near the several train stops, according to Margaret who says, "the only things on the other side of Butler were the police station and a big convict camp near the water tower where the prisoners, wearing balls and chains, slept in tents."

Margaret was devoted to her father and decided early on she wanted to be a journalist just like him. She says he worked until he was 76. He passed away in 1952 immediately after writing his final newspaper editorial.

Margaret went to school through the third grade on Tybee, attending classes in a one-room schoolhouse where most students went to school barefoot.

"Then my father decided we needed civilizing, so we moved into Savannah, but kept a house at the beach," she says, and it was there that she spent the summers of her youth.

In the early 1920s, she says Sunday afternoons in Savannah featured family excursions out to Wilmington Island in the car to check on the progress of the road being built to Tybee.

Margaret, who remains an attractive, meticulously coiffed woman with a quick wit and ready smile, always had a string of suitors in high school.

"But back then we weren't allowed to date just one boy," she smiles. "You could go out on Friday and Saturday night, but it had to be with different people. Our parents didn't want us to get serious about anyone, and there was safety in numbers."

Despite such precautions, one of the boys she dated became quite smitten with her.

"When I was out with another boy, he would drink a bit too much and come over to my house," she says. "Mom would put him to sleep in the maid's room and call his mother and let her know he was all right."

"Boys didn't drink when they were on a date, but when they went to dances stag they did, and many would wind up at the police station."

Margaret Palmer discusses world travels over coffee.

Most of her summer dates on Tybee were spent on the old pavilion listening to famous big bands like Bob Crosby and his Bobcats and Harry James, and dancing to swing and shag numbers.

Margaret still likes to shag and is delighted to see that Tybee's new pavilion is once more becoming a focal point for the island.

"I wondered if that would ever happen again," she says. "It's not quite the same, but then there's a different generation now, and back then there was the grand old Tybee Hotel nearby."

Many parents also attended the dances, forming a large circle sitting in rocking chairs while keeping a sharp eye on their youngsters to make sure they didn't stray out of sight behind the bandstand.

"My folks were quite strict about my getting home on time," she says. "I had to be home by midnight, and we lived near Lovell Station, just across from the old water tower. I'd leave the dance and run all the way home barefoot, holding my sandals and my long organdy dress up as I ran, with my date running along beside me."

She also enjoyed strolling along the wooden beachside boardwalk and attending the movies in the modern new theater at Fort Screven.

Sometimes, she says, she would spend time watching the convicts cleaning along the railroad tracks while still chained to one another.

Margaret says she loved the train ride out from the city but flinches when she recalls the hot cinders blowing in through the windows and burning holes in passengers' clothing.

"The track ran right down Butler Avenue, but there was no street there then," she recalls. "It would continue to the south end of the island where it would be turned around to head back toward Savannah."

After completing high school in the city, she headed for the University of Georgia, still bent on becoming a journalist.

Margaret says she got the chance of a lifetime when she was selected to be an exchange student at the University of Heidelberg in Germany for her senior year.

While attending college in Heidelberg, Hitler, who was nearing the peak of his power with the Third Reich in 1938, came to the city and agreed to be interviewed by Margaret.

Mesmerized by Hitler's penetrating, "sky blue eyes and dynamic presence," Margaret says, "all my journalistic training went right out the window."

"He was very imposing and every time I asked a question, he turned it around and interviewed me about my thoughts on Germany and how I found life there. I came out having sat and talked with him for about 45 minutes but with no real interview."

Just out of her teens and impressionable, Margaret admits she was awed, and was particularly impressed by Hitler's emphasis on youth and the empowerment he bestowed on Germany's young people.

"It was so different than it had been at the University of Georgia where I lived in a sorority house and the main concern was who you were going to attend the next dance with," she says. "People my age in Germany were serious. It was hard not to get swept up and go along with them."

Entranced by the excitement of the events there, she joined Hitler's youth movement because of its vitality and camaraderie and the fact that membership enabled her to travel and stay in youth hostels for 15 cents a night.

"I loved the German people," she says. "I still stay in touch with many I met during those days."

When her sister came over on vacation, bringing $500 to finance a visit to Paris, Margaret convinced her they should use the money to purchase a motorcycle and tour Europe while saving money by spending their nights at those hostels.

They covered 2,100 miles during her sister's month-long visit.

Margaret says it was clear at the time that Germany was about to invade Austria and, ever curious and already having a journalist's eye for a story, she wanted to be there when it happened.

She traveled to Vienna by train, "and I was there when Hitler marched in," she says.

While she was witnessing history, the Germans closed the border, leaving her stranded in a small hotel they had confiscated for use as a barracks.

It was only after negotiations conducted through the U.S. Embassy that she was she able extricate herself. Margaret spoke German fluently and was readily accepted by German friends (she dated "a delightful young man who was a member of the SS," she says) who felt they were paying her the highest of complements when they suggested that she must really be a German rather than American.

The impression she gleaned from these friends was that Germans simply wanted to regain the African colonies taken from them following World War I, along with the Sudetenland portion of Czechoslovakia.

"The Nazi regime thought any German-speaking people needed to be incorporated into the homeland," she says.

It was only later that Margaret learned there was a much darker side to Hitler and his regime.

After graduation, she got her first job in the office of the U.S. Consul General in Hamburg, "and it was there that I got a little maturity and began to understand what was going on," she recalls.

She was in Hamburg on the infamous "Kristallnacht" when Hitler's followers ran amok breaking windows in Jewish businesses and homes throughout the city.

"I was sent out to report on it for the consulate and it was terrible," she says.

She also witnessed the frenzied efforts of German Jews to escape the country by immigrating to the United States.

"Hundreds of thousands of them came to the Hamburg seaport trying to get out, but most of them didn't have a quota number high enough, and U.S. quotas were very strict," she says. "My job was to interview them when they came in for a quota number."

"A lot of them committed suicide in the streets because they knew there was no way to get out. It was an eye opener. It was so sad."

She remained with the consulate until all American civilians were ordered to leave the country just prior to the U.S. becoming involved in the war.

"I thought it was a European conflict, but things happened so fast!" she says. "I was aboard a ship between Hamburg and Southampton when the war broke out on Sept. 3, 1939."

After two-and-a-half years in Germany, Margaret returned to her parents' home in Savannah, but lingered only briefly before Secretary of State Cordell Hull offered her a position with the State Department in Washington.

She was so delighted with the work, she decided to forego journalism for a career in the Foreign Service and was immediately assigned to the U.S. embassy in Mexico.

That's where she met her husband, Joseph Palmer, a native of Boston who was the vice consul on his initial posting with the Foreign Service.

They were married in 1941 at the Cathedral of St. John the Baptist in Savannah. That ended Margaret's Foreign Service career because women at the time were required to resign when they married.

"I remember reading the letters from our families just before our wedding," Margaret laughs. "Mine said, with all the nice Southern boys I knew, they never thought I would marry a Yankee."

"His asked why, with all those nice New England girls, he would marry a Southerner. I think they pictured some flibberty thing like Scarlet O'Hara. In those days it was almost like a mixed marriage."

Joseph was appointed vice consul in charge of the U.S. embassy in Nairobi, East Africa, where he became an expert on the Dark Continent. The two spent 20 years in various postings there, during which time "we fell in love with Africa," says Margaret.

"At the time there were no such things as safaris. We had animals like giraffes and zebras in our garden, and our only concern was when lions would approach the town. Officials alerted residents and they would take extra care with their children when they sent them out to play."

Shortly after arriving in Africa, Margaret says she sat on a beach on the continent's west coast gazing across the water. "Tybee is over there," she said to herself as she recalled those evenings with her father, looking towards Africa.

Margaret and Joseph returned to Tybee on vacations a number of times during his extended service in Africa.

"Wherever I was, whenever I was troubled, I always felt things would be all right if I could just get back to Tybee," she smiles. "This place is just good for your soul."

Joseph became a full ambassador when they were assigned to Nigeria, which won its independence during his tour.

Margaret relaxes in her Tybee home.

"Nigeria was my favorite country," says Margaret. "It's hot. It smells bad. It's noisy and raucous, but it's the most wonderful place because of the people. They're so easy and beautiful and tall, and the women in Nigeria run everything! The blacks in Savannah are very much like those in Nigeria, very tall and very strong and dark."

"That was a very exciting time. Kennedy was president, and we saw the first Peace Corps people arrive. Those were the great years! Countries all over the continent started becoming independent."

Both Ted and Bobby Kennedy visited with the Palmers during that time, but her favorite guest was TV newsman Edward R. Murrow.

"He was fascinating and very quiet and all he required was an endless supply of coffee," she recalls. "He was a real doll. Of course, he also smoked constantly, but he was a wonderful man, very deep and intelligent. He was a newspaperman's newspaperman."

One of the many highlights she experienced during the Nigeria posting came on the night of her arrival by boat when Joseph, who had come to the country weeks before, informed her that she must prepare immediately to attend a formal ball.

"I didn't know a soul at the ball, and my husband was off networking when a tall black man invited me to dance," she says.

The band was playing West African tunes, and her partner complemented her on her ability to dance to this music.

Each initially assumed the other was a native to Nigeria, but during their conversation they discovered both had been born in Savannah.

He was the son of the former pastor of the West Broad Street Baptist Church who had served with Margaret's father on the board of the Bethesda Home.

"What do you think our parents would say if they could look down now and see us dancing?" her partner, then a lawyer in New York, asked.

"I hope they would both be happy," she replied. "I do, too," he agreed.

"That was a magic moment," she says.

Just prior to his retirement, Joseph was serving as assistant secretary of state when he was offered his choice of embassies for his final assignment.

He and Margaret decided on North Africa since they had served in virtually every other area on the continent and wanted to round out their experiences.

Shortly after their arrival in Tripoli, Muammar Qadhafi took power, making their assignment far less pleasant than the Mediterranean sojourn they had visualized.

"It was really pretty grim," she says, recalling that her impression of Qadhafi is that "he is xenophobic but he's definitely not crazy. He's smart. I think his mentor was Nasser, and so he's very fiery Arabic. Libya is a strange but interesting country."

Because of the revolutionary atmosphere, Margaret was not permitted to go out after 9 at night, making it difficult for her to make friends with the residents, as she had at all their previous postings.

"We had a wall around our compound, and no one was permitted to visit with us," she laments.

During that four-year tour, Joseph's principal assignment was to negotiate the closing of the large U.S. Air Force Base in Libya.

Diplomatic relations deteriorated during their stay, and ultimately only seven people remained on the embassy staff, which had numbered 130 when they arrived.

After completing that tour, they returned to Washington where Joseph retired in 1973.

Following an extended debate about where to reside in retirement, they decided to live between their home in Bethesda, Md., and Tybee Island, where they purchased a cottage.

From early spring "up until the time it really gets hot in early July," she says, they lived on Tybee, then returned to Bethesda for the remainder of the year.

Margaret has continued this practice since Joseph's death five years ago.

"I love it here," she says. "It's so peaceful, and the people here are so kind and accepting, and I love the beach. I do a lot of walking there, and I enjoy going out to the beach to sit, usually late in the afternoon."

"Tybee is a good place to be from and a great place to come back to."

One of her sons, Joe Palmer, who was born during one of their tours in Africa, now resides on the island's north end and works in the construction business.

POSTSCRIPT: Margaret McCamy Jones Palmer passed away in her Bethesda, Md. home on Aug. 23, 2013. She was 96.

Capt. Clifford Boyd -

Independent Captain Going Strong

A Man
By Land
Or Sea

*H*e's lived off the land, made his living from the sea and, though 70 now, he's still never far from either.

They call him the captain, although he's pretty much hove to these days at his spread on Wilmington Island, where his property seems to run a country mile from the main road on out through the marsh to the river beyond.

It's a wide swath of land he's had for years that has now become so valuable he's constantly pestered by hungry realtors who'd love to acquire it.

But you can tell from the set of Capt. Clifford Boyd's jaw and the steely look in his eyes when he discusses such would-be interlopers that they'll have to hanker for it quite a while before they get their hands on it.

Capt. Boyd, the patriarch of an extensive clan of Boyds on the island, acquired the property in 1970 after having roamed the area in his youth, when you could still hunt and fish anywhere on Wilmington and never be bothered by those pesky city folks.

"Used to go out to the islands," he says, while scanning the hammocks rising above the marsh grass in the distance. "I'd drop a buck 'n drag him home to eat. Didn't have to worry much about huntin' seasons back then. Now they'd arrest you for pointin' a BB gun the wrong way."

The captain seems completely contented hunkered down in his marshfront home, but you won't find him there during the hunting season or when the fish are running.

He has just returned from three months of deer hunting on 1,300 acres of woods and swamp up around Clio, just north of Savannah.

He goes there every year to camp out with some friends in an old school bus, then heads out from the bus on his four-wheel-drive ATV, driving several miles deep into the swamp to hunt.

Capt. Boyd brought back a buck and a doe on this trip. Most of his other good ole boy buddies who were out there with him weren't as lucky this time.

The captain now rides a wheelchair to get around at home as a result of a stroke he suffered five years ago.

"Knocked me down when the damned thing hit me, but I pinched myself and I could feel it," he says, matter-of-factly. "I said damn, I ain't dead so I've got to get some help."

He was alone at the time, as he mostly is nowadays, and found he couldn't stand, walk or crawl.

"Had to slide across the floor on my back and when I got to the phone, I pulled it down on the floor. I was able to punch the numbers. Called my niece, and then I couldn't talk, just mumbled."

His devoted niece, Joyce Fisher, recognized his mumble and sent an ambulance to rush him to the hospital where he remained for about three months.

"They told me how fortunate I was and all that," says the captain, frowning with the recollection.

Shortly afterward, he underwent open heart surgery and has been confined to the wheelchair ever since.

With his eyes twinkling beneath his knit navy watch cap, he still looks like the weathered sea captain of bygone days, and given his hearty handshake and gregarious smile you don't notice that wheelchair after a while.

The captain's no stranger to adversity.

He had polio shortly after he was born that left him with a limp, and he was abandoned by his parents when he was just ten months old to be raised by his grandparents and an aunt.

"Looked up my mother and father later on, but I wasn't too impressed," he says. "My aunt was my real mother. She adopted me."

The captain says his parents never explained their action, "but I ain't hung up about it. The only time I think about it is when somebody like you comes along and wants to talk."

He's only alone by choice these days, however.

Up until about four months ago, Capt. Boyd had a female friend living with him "but she smoked so much I could hardly breathe in the house. I told my niece about it and she hung a big 'No Smoking' sign on the front door."

The woman left. The sign remains.

"That was alright with me, too," he says. "She still calls me once 'n a while. Still has her hook out for me. But she wasn't quite my type. I wasn't ready to get nailed down, you know?"

"She's lookin' to marry. Wanted me to sign everything over to her in advance. I don't need that. She damned sure had plans. I can get along fine without a girlfriend."

The captain took up fishing as a youngster with his older cousin, Marion Boyd, who operated three charter boats on the Wilmington River.

He started taking fishing parties out on his own when

he was just 14, cruising 25 miles out to Black Fish
Banks off the Carolina/Georgia coast.

"We'd mostly do bottom fishing and some trolling for
Spanish mackerel," he says.

When he turned 16, he bought into his own charter
boat and got his license "making it all legal."

Later, the captain began ferrying yachts for wealthy
owners from New York to Miami.

"I'd take 'em down in the fall and bring 'em back in
the spring," he says. "It was a good life. I enjoyed it."

He also got married along the way, and he took a
break to pursue his other love, camping out in the
woods.

He and his wife, Dottie, hunkered down on Daufuskie
Island where they sustained themselves by hunting
and fishing and doing a little shrimping.

"We just lived off the land," he says. "We both hunt-
ed. She could keep up with me. Liked doing everything I like to do."

"I did some shrimping and sold a bunch, and we had
a garden. We got along fine, and she was a damned
good cook."

Capt. Boyd says his wife was particularly good at
preparing venison, which is one of his favorite dishes.
Now he cooks up his own. He especially likes it when

he's up in the woods hunting.

"Food tastes better up there," he says.

His recipe for fresh venison is to "slice it thin, beat some flour into it and throw it in hot grease. Just don't overcook it. That's good eatin'."

Reflecting on his Daufuskie days, he says only nine Whites and 138 Blacks were living there during his stay and things were right primitive, but they got a bit easier when electricity was run out to the island.

After living on the island for three years the captain, armed with only a high school diploma ("I ain't into college educatin"), became Daufuskie's magistrate.

He took the job when his grandfather, the former magistrate and lighthouse keeper for the Bloody Point Light on Daufuskie, "got to where he couldn't hear the cases and had me set up for it."

Asked what he did to prepare for the position, the captain chuckles and responds: "I didn't do nothin."

He does admit that his grandfather gave him a set of books on South Carolina law and was available for advice when he needed it.

"I did a good bit of readin' in that damned code of laws," he recalls. "I enjoyed it 'cause mostly all I'd do is fish and hunt. I had so few cases that you couldn't even call any of 'em a case."

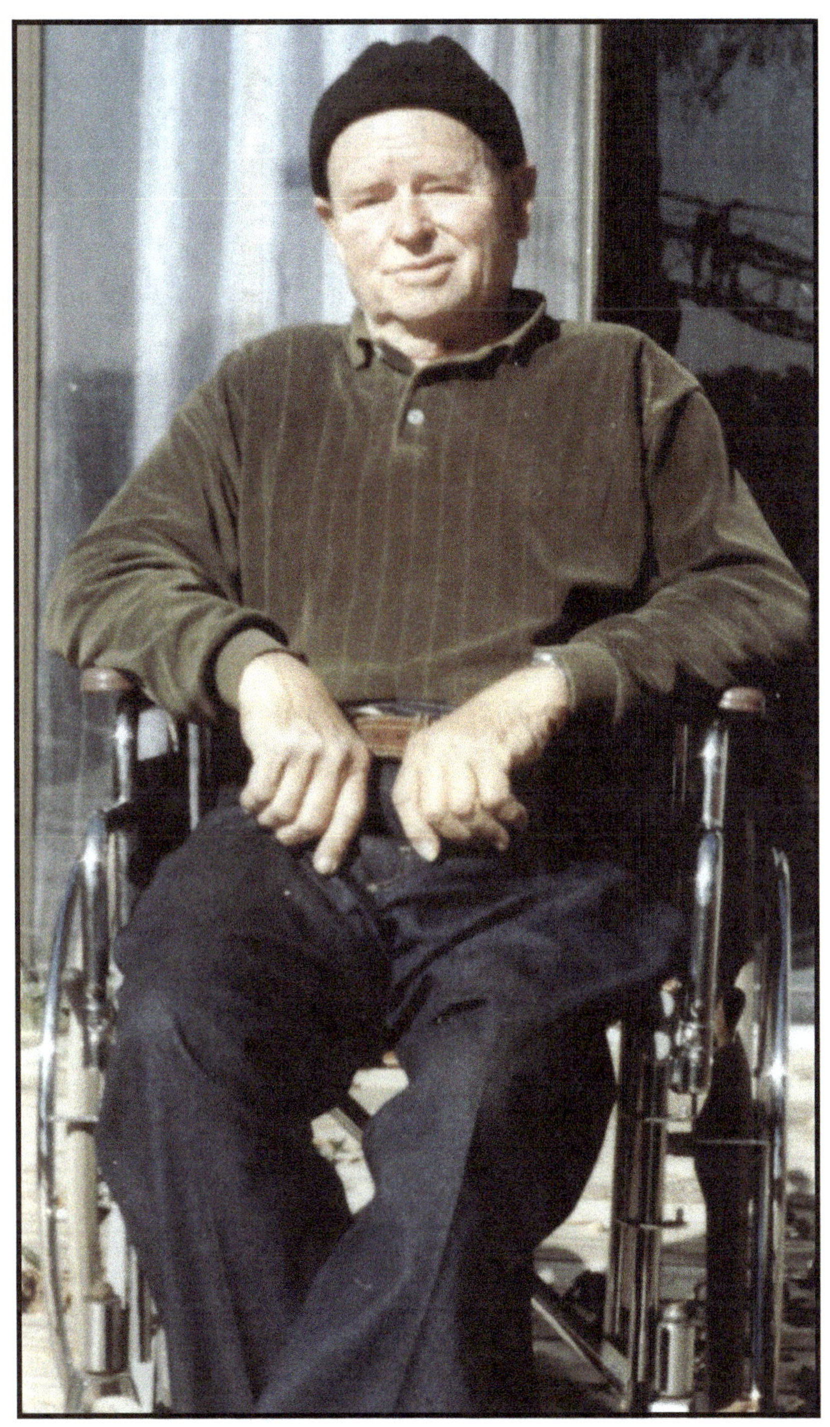

Captain Clifford Boyd.

"Didn't have anything complicated. Common law wives beatin' on each other, you know, just child's stuff. No murders. Nothing like that. Drinkin' and pouring potash on somebody. Stuff like that."

The stiffest sentence he meted out was when "a guy threatened to kill somebody and I believed him."

"That's the only one I sent to jail. He was there about a month. They took him and dried him out, sobered him up, and let him go."

The captain bought five acres of land on the water and built a house with his own hands while he was the magistrate.

"I used wood from another old house I tore down," he says. "Built a dock, too."

He purchased the property for $4,000 and later "sold it to my old shipmate for $9,000 in 1968, when he wanted to retire there, and he did. Lived there 'til he died. Wish I had that land now. It'd be worth somethin'."

The captain says he ran into some interesting people on Daufuskie.

There was "Fast Man," for one. "He was called the island messenger. He'd deliver a message to one end of the island and be back with an answer before you knew he was gone."

"You couldn't say he was walking, and you couldn't

say he was running. He was just moving his feet real good."

And there was another man who spent most of his time trying to keep the island clean.

"He was hung up on cleaning," says Capt. Boyd. "He was always picking up litter and beer cans and stuff."

That man was killed when he wandered off the island while continuing to pursue his penchant for tidiness.

"He was over on Hilton Head, leaning over by the road to pick up some trash when he was hit by a big black car," according to Capt. Boyd, who says he doesn't recall anyone ever being charged in that case.

After two years of "magistratin'," the captain figured he could make a better living in the oil fields of south Texas and headed there to improve his economic status when an uncle wrote that he had work for him as a mechanic.

"I liked that area, down around Corpus Christi," he says. "Used to run out to Padre Island. It was beautiful. We'd fish and shoot jackrabbits on the beach."

His wife liked Texas too.

"No matter where we went or what we did we was happy," he says.

He and Dottie returned to Wilmington after three years because the work got to be too much for him.

"I couldn't handle it very well, crawling around those oil rigs with my bad leg," he says.

Shortly after their return from Texas, he was hired by prominent Savannah banker Mills B. Lane to work on the Flying Lady, a 62-foot Trumpy yacht the banker kept moored in Savannah.

He served as a mate for three years before being named captain when the former captain, his cousin Marion Boyd, retired.

The new Capt. Boyd remained in that position for the next 17 years, ferrying Lane and his friends and business associates around area waters and down to Miami and back.

He made that trip during the Democratic Convention in Miami where Governor (later President) Jimmy Carter came aboard with other dignitaries.

The captain also took Carter to Harbour Town on Hilton Head and on other trips before he became president.

"And I entertained Lords and Ladies from England, all of 'em guests of the C&S Bank," which Mills Lane operated.

"Those were good times. I enjoyed that. I really liked those people."

"The bigger people are regular people. They're awful nice."

"The in between people, the strugglers trying to get there, I didn't care for some of them."

Occasionally, when his mate or the bartender/cook ("the bartender was the most important of all of us," he laughs) failed to show up, Capt. Boyd would get his wife Dottie to serve as mate.

"She enjoyed that too, like everything else we did together," he recalls.

The captain stepped down from his post aboard the Flying Lady ten years ago. Then Dottie died last March. They'd been married for 34 years.

Now the captain stays busy "huntin', fishin' and doin' a little trav-lin'. Sometimes I go down to Florida to play the dogs. Stuff like that."

Currently, he's contemplating the coming fishing season.

"Got a 21-foot Boston Whaler with a 200 Evinrude on it," he says.

He'll be making his old run out to the Black Fish Banks and plans to keep doing that for a while but is now giving serious consideration to taking a companion along.

"It's gettin' kind of hard to keep the boat up," he says. "They're a lot of work and goin' down there and crawlin' in and out is gettin' harder."

"I figure I'll have to give up the fishin' before the huntin'. Plan to keep doing that. As long as I've got my Jeep to haul the four-wheeler up there, I'll still be able to make it."

"As long as I'm able to go, I'm gonna go. I don't need nothin' else."

POST SCRIPT: Capt. Clifford M. Boyd passed away on Jan. 15, 2005 in Hospice Savannah. He was 78-years-old.

Albert Williams Jr. -
He's Been There and Done That

Recalling Tugs and All That Jazz

*H*e's one of the good ol' island boys who's been into and done most of the things on Tybee that have become the stuff of melancholy memories.

Albert M. Williams Jr., known to everyone hereabouts simply as "Rooster," has floated for hours on the Back River; worked as a lifeguard while chasing girls on the south end beach; played drums with famous musicians; operated his own bar; served as merchant mariner; worked aboard tugs, and been a stalwart participant in sundry island shenanigans.

He was back in the limelight helping to open Tybee's tourist season recently when he served as Grand Marshal and drew cheers along the entire route of the 13th annual Beach Bum Parade.

Rooster, who hadn't seen daylight yet, was transported from Tybee to Savannah for his birth but immediately beat a path back to bury his roots deep in the island's sand.

His unusual nickname was bestowed on him at the tender age of 2 by the then colorful Tybee Police Chief W. W. "High Pockets" Edwards, who was a buddy of Rooster's father, a master mechanic whom legendary local lawyer Sonny Seiler christened "Motor Doctor" because he could instantly diagnose the trouble with any engine he got his hands on.

Since High Pockets, who was so dubbed because his exceedingly long legs placed his pockets unusually high up, was the only cop on the island, Rooster's Dad helped him out occasionally and they spent a lot of time riding their big Harley motorcycles around the island.

Back in those days, folks sometimes failed to call on the law to deal with undesirables.

According to old timers, troublemakers got dumped on the far side of the Lazaretto Creek Bridge in their "birthday suits" with instructions to head toward Savannah and never look back.

They say real ornery types were sometimes hauled to Goat Island, where they were stripped and tied to a tree for an overnight stay with the mosquitoes, unless they were notorious miscreants. Those got a dose of honey over their bodies as extra enticement for ants and other insects.

Some swear such stiff justice was far more effective than the penalties meted out by today's more civilized court system because the bad guys invariably got the message and repeat offenders were noticeable only by their absence.

"It's too bad the place has changed," says Rooster.

In any event, 2-year-old Albert was hoisted behind
High Pockets on his Harley one day and when the
chief pulled to a stop by the old water tower (the new
one is in the same location) he saw tears streaming
down the boy's face.

"That boy's cryin' like a rooster," said the chief.

That was back in 1937 and Albert's been "Rooster"
ever since.

Rooster claims his tears were prompted because his
foot was badly burned on the motorcycle's exhaust
and "I've still got a scar there."

Life was simple back then for young Rooster, who rol-
licked through his teens on Tybee fishing, crabbing,
and swimming.

"I spent 99 percent of my time on the beach as a
kid," he says. "I'd swim all day. We didn't have much
when I was a boy, and I didn't have any shoes until
I was in junior high school. You didn't need any on
Tybee."

He hung out at the old icehouse on Inlet Avenue,
where he and other youngsters wiled away summer
afternoons.

"There was always something cookin' there, always

something going on," he says, smiling as he savors the memory.

Some of the kids picked up pocket money working at the icehouse. The boys were sometimes exhausted from muscling around 300-pound blocks of ice, but they found it a cool place to work on hot August afternoons.

When Rooster reached his mid-teens, he joined his buddies as a lifeguard on the beach at the south end of the island, where he became quite a ladies' man when he served as head lifeguard for a couple of years.

"There weren't many out there that I didn't catch," he says of the dozens of female tourists who crowded around his guard's stand. "I dated some good lookin' women."

Rooster sometimes spent entire afternoons floating along the Back River with his friends.

"We'd get in at flood tide on the point on the south end and float along half a day, all the way to the fishing camp up the river, sometimes stopping off on mud flats to rest a while," he says.

"We never used any life vests or anything like that. If the tide turned and we couldn't get back, we'd walk up to the road and thumb a ride back to the beach."

Rooster had his first drink of hard liquor in the old Brass Rail bar when he was 17.

"They'd let lifeguards in there free," he smiles.

The pier, the Brass Rail, and other bars along what was then 16th street were as magnetic as the bathing beauties for Rooster, but it wasn't the booze. It was the music that attracted him.

Famous big bands frequently played on the pier when it was converted from day use as a skating rink to a dance floor at night and you could generally find Rooster there or at one of the bars in the area where the sweet sounds of music oozed out onto the street.

Band leader Dean Hudson staged a talent show on the pier, which Rooster entered when he was five years old.

"I came in second singing Mares Eat Oats and Does Eat Oats," he laughs.

But it was the big band, West Coast and New York jazz music he was irresistibly drawn to.

He got to know many of the most prominent jazz musicians in the country and frequently followed their performances from coast to coast.

Popular songstress Anita O'Day became a close friend, and he rambled through jazz-filled evenings with her and other famous musicians.

Rooster assembled a massive collection of jazz re-cords, many of which he still owns and plays in his home. Unfortunately, many of his rare records were

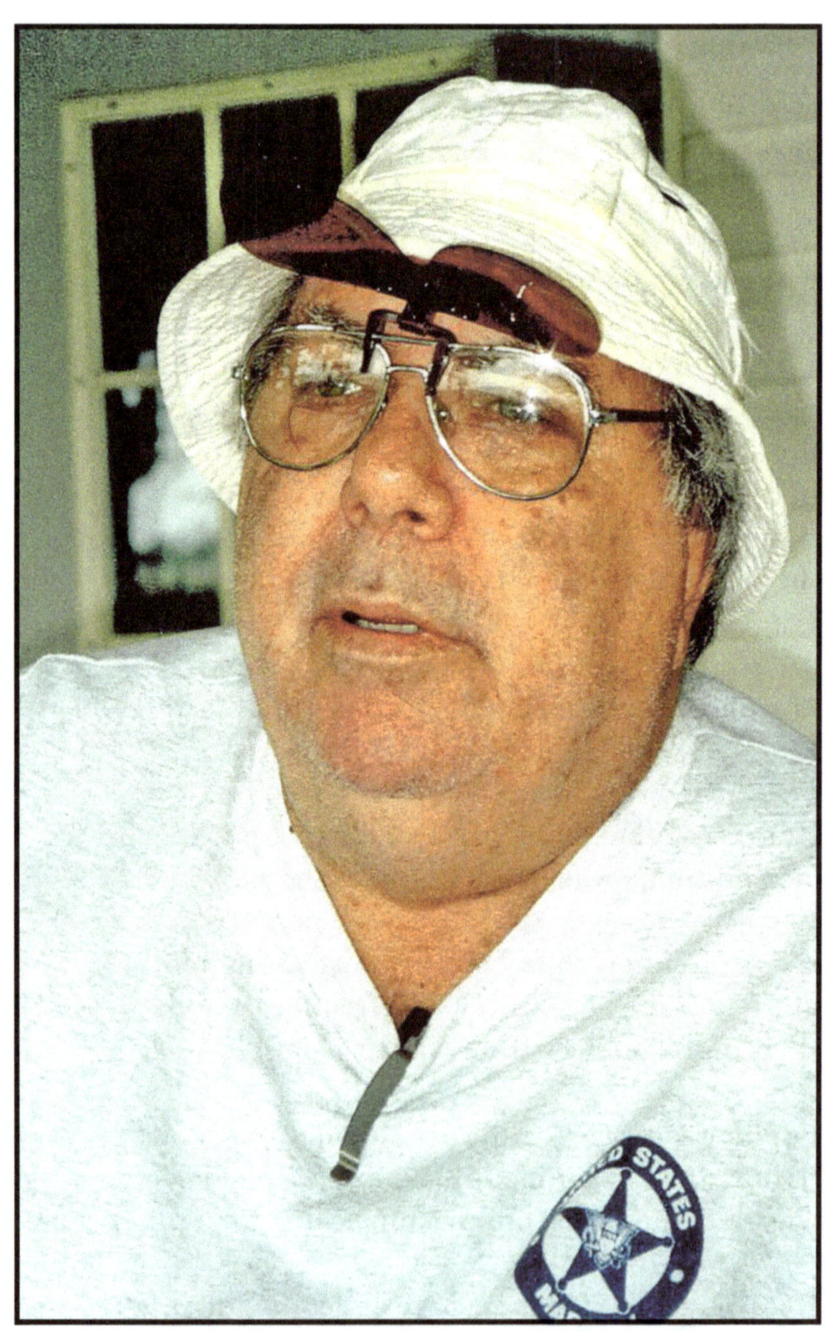

Rooster Williams remembers the good old days.

lost in a house fire, but he still has a fine collection which his son keeps urging him to record on CD's. Rooster became an accomplished drummer, learning by playing along with his records. He performed on River Street in Savannah with his good friend, legendary local musician Kenny Palmer.

Bongos and conga drums were his favorites, his idol being Cuban drummer Chano Pozo whose records he collected.

"He was the best there was," claims Rooster. "He came here in the early part of 1947 playing with Dizzy Gillespie in New York, but he was into drugs bad."

"He was killed in a bar in Manhattan, blown right off his bar stool. Anybody who plays congas or bongos who never heard of him, they don't know anybody."

While still in his early 20s, Rooster operated the Red Barn bar at Butler and 16th Street, which he rented from Willie Haar, who owned the Brass Rail and several other Tybee night spots.

Rooster says Haar also operated a rum-running boat operating out of Thunderbolt.

Back in the Prohibition days, the families of many now reputable area residents were involved in such operations in Thunderbolt as well as on Wilmington and other nearby islands.

The Red Barn specialized in jazz music that Rooster himself selected for the juke box.

"Not many people danced there," he recalls. "They'd just come in to listen to the music. That was a lot of fun."

He still gets a bit melancholy reflecting on those melodious evenings and says he wouldn't mind opening another bar if he could find the right spot with the right music and sound system.

Even now Rooster travels as far as Miami to catch a performance by a first-rate jazz band "but there are not many left," he laments.

His real ambition as a teen was to land a high-paying job aboard a tug on Savannah's waterfront, but those positions were almost impossible to come by.

"I started bugging them from the time I was 17 about working on a tug," he says.

When a tug operator said his chances would be enhanced if he had some experience on ships, Rooster signed up with the Merchant Marine and sailed the coast aboard freighters when business dried up at his bar in the off season.

During stopovers in New York, he frequented famous jazz clubs like Birdland and the Cafe Bohemia, where he got to know the musicians and sometimes crossed the country to attend their performances in San Francisco.

After a couple of years at sea he was able to land that coveted job aboard a tug in 1962 and spent the next

25 years nudging ships into and out of their berths on the Savannah River.

"That was a real dream job," he says. "Everybody wanted to get a job there. The pay was good, and it had good conditions. Everything was so good."

Following retirement, he chased down bail jumpers for a bonding company for a couple of years, becoming involved in some tense situations "but it was a lot of fun," he says.

Throughout his working life, Rooster continued to run with lifelong buddies on Tybee, sometimes hitting the road with them when sprinklings of lingering wanderlust lured him on spur-of-the-moment adventures.

The owner of the icehouse operated a trucking business in the off season, and Rooster sometimes hauled tomatoes with him from Florida north for several days at a time for both business and pleasure.

"You know those guys who say they've been there and done that?" he asks. "Well, unless they've walked in my sneakers, I don't think they have. I've been there, and I did it."

Like most islanders who have been around long enough, Rooster has had his share of minor rubs with the power structure.

He describes how he was able to get the undivided attention of city council members when he was having trouble with the sewerage lines leading to his house.

"I got me a clear, five-gallon bucket and put some water and paper and stuff in it with a plastic bag on top and took it to a council meeting. I said this looks like a five-gallon bucket, but we use it as a slop jar because the sewerage is so bad. You keep it."

When the city refused to place stop signs at a nearby intersection, Rooster roamed the island picking up stop signs which had been knocked over.

"I read the DOT rules and all where they said a municipality has to put up stop signs and they didn't, even though council voted to put up four signs there, so I put up four stop signs, none of 'em the right height or nothing."

His last tiff with the council involved a big old diesel motor Rooster hung from a tree in his yard. His intention had been to repair the thing and make a few bucks, but he never got around to it, and the city pressed him to take it down.

"They raised hell with me for a long time, and I told them that was okay, but the property was posted, and they'd better not come on it."

Ultimately the city removed the motor.

"The funny thing was that I got that motor from the city to begin with, and they hauled it back and dumped it right where I got it," he laughs.

Rooster says the biggest problem on the island now is "too many people."

"Too many people want to run the island that aren't even registered voters. If you're not even a registered voter, don't even talk to me. If you can't cast your vote, you don't mean nothing to me."

"I don't support any of those jackleg folks that's in there now. There's too many people that don't have a say-so that are saying something, and people are listening to 'em. Leave things the way they were."

"I tell people, if you don't like it here, please go somewhere else. Why'd you leave where you were? Go to Wilmington or Savannah or move to Hilton Head. Taxes are real reasonable in South Carolina."

"And what makes me really sick is the way the taxes are going up. The taxes on my house are higher now than my monthly payment was."

Despite his views on the current state of the island, however, Rooster seems to have mellowed a bit and slowed down a step or two in his stroll toward seasoned citizen status.

"I've had a real fulfilling life, got a good wife, and been married 37 years, and two good kids and never any real trouble but work was maybe the best part of it," he says. "I miss working."

Several major back operations have curtailed Rooster's mobility and since he's not what you'd call a morning person, a regular 9 to 5 position would be out of the question.

"I won't do much of anything before noon, won't even go in for doctor's appointments in the morning when they schedule me then," he says. "I worked for years being on call 24 hours a day and getting up to go at all hours, and now I sleep when I want to."

His aversion to pre-noon activities may also stem from his status as one of Tybee's true night owls.

Doc's Bar, where he hunkers down on a corner stool most nights and into the early morning hours, is a favorite haunt. Rooster has become a fixture there making new friends and drawing dozens of island buddies over to share tales of the good old days and listen to the music he loves.

"Charlie's (house musician Charlie Sherrill) pretty good," he says. "He plays good flute. I really love a good flute."

Rooster's eyes still sparkle when he discusses the possibility of serving up such music, albeit a bit heavier on classic jazz, in his own place once again.

Yeah, says Rooster, "it would be just like the good old days."

POSTSCRIPT: Albert M. "Rooster" Williams Jr. passed away on July 2, 2004. He was 68 years old.

Anne Monaghan -
Lone Lady Wins Tybee Council Post

Big Voice,
Big Smile and
Big Plans for Island

*I*t was her first run for elective office, and in a field of 21 candidates for six Tybee City Council seats she won handily.

Now Anne Monaghan will be the lone lady on the island's new council, but that doesn't bother her at all.

She grew up and had a successful career in what was considered mostly men's domain, which makes working with a mayor and five male council members seem natural.

"I don't even think about it that way," she says. "In my career I've never been caught up in that, never even thought about being a woman."

"I just look at myself as a person I hope can contribute to the council, not because I'm a woman but because I'm Anne Monaghan."

"I didn't have a platform as such. I had a vision that

Anne Monaghan conducts art auction in City Hall for charity.

we could make a working team on council, and I still feel that way."

Her initial goals are to gain a thorough knowledge of city affairs, meet the needs of the island's senior citizens who she believes have been shortchanged on Tybee, and take action to preserve the island's picturesque appearance.

The learning process poses no problem for Anne. She enjoys assimilating new information and has had a long and distinguished career in education.

She's already off and running in her effort to ensure

that the island's seniors have a wider variety of satisfying activities by spearheading what she terms "a low-key effort" to organize Tybee's senior citizens, determine their interests and fulfill their needs.

But don't call them "senior citizens," laughs Anne.

At her initial meeting with older residents, a spry 85-year-old claimed members don't want to be thought of as "senior citizens" and suggested the group be called "YEEPIE," an acronym for "Young, Energetic, Enthusiastic, People Interested in Everything."

That name was endorsed enthusiastically by the 25 people in attendance.

There was considerable talk at the formative meeting about what the members could do for others and how they might help with the city's proposed new master plan.

"The more mature people on the island want to be involved with more than just knitting and quilting," says Anne. "They're not interested in just going out line dancing."

Anne got an early start dealing with male majorities. Her two siblings are older brothers.

"I was the kid sister tomboy," she smiles, noting that she played football as a child and later became an avid tennis player and enthusiastic sailor.

"I love my brothers," she says. "They're just wonderful."

But she admits they did complicate her early social
life because her prospective boyfriends had to under-
go intense scrutiny and endless questions from her
brothers "who could really be intimidating."

Anne says she knew those who made it through her
brothers' gauntlet were sincerely interested in her.

Born in Andover, Mass., her father was a leather company executive "who was one of the last real leather
experts in the country," she says. Her mother immigrated to Boston from Ireland as a teenager.

Anne finished grade and prep school in Andover,
Mass., then earned her degree in Education at Rose-
mount College in Philadelphia.

After four years of teaching in Northern Virginia
elementary schools, she took two months off to tour
Europe during which she visited relatives in Ireland.

"That was very, very special," she says of her initial
trip to Ireland.

"My mother came from a family of seven on a peat
farm. They call it farming peat there, you cut it out
of the earth. I had an uncle who did not speak a word
of English, just pure Gaelic. That was fascinating."

A keepsake from her mother's homeland, the trunk
she brought with her when she immigrated, is dis-

played prominently in the foyer of Anne's Tybee home.

Anne feels that sabbatical and the subsequent ones she took through the years made her a more effective teacher and administrator, noting, "I always said I was going to do my traveling up front. It's something you should do when you're still young and can really enjoy it."

Following her European sojourn, Anne was hired to do research correspondence with National Geographic in Washington, D.C.

"I really liked that," she says. "It was a fun job. When I started out, I wanted to be in journalism but the college I attended offered only one course in communications so that was impossible."

After departing National Geographic, she landed what she terms "a wonderful job at the White House" working on President Kennedy's social staff.

"It was Camelot, just a wonderful experience to have," she says. "Can you imagine anything better than to walk into the White House every morning and have people salute you! It was good stuff."

Anne then returned to teaching in Fairfax, Va. but that seemed rather pale when compared with her earlier experiences.

Wanting more, she worked on her master's degree evenings and during the summer at the University of

Virginia in order to become a school administrator, a goal she realized far earlier than she anticipated.

Anne became a school principal in Virginia several months before she had even received her degree.

"I really loved being a principal," she says. "In those days you could be an instructional leader without the interference you experience today."

That interference stems mostly from "the parents who changed over the years," she says. They either became disinterested in their children's schooling "or became over-interested to the point that their little darlings could do no wrong."

She cited a recent news story about teachers being reprimanded for correcting two 5-year-olds for throwing away food after having been instructed not to take more than they would eat as an example of changing times.

"The parents went all the way to the sheriff's department" to complain about the teachers, she says. "I read that and said this is exactly what we're talking about" when referring to the deteriorating role of educators.

"Don't ask schools to teach values if you don't have them yourself," Anne admonishes. "It's taking the whole emphasis away from what we did well."

"I get annoyed when I hear people condemning the public school system. I spent over 30 years of my life

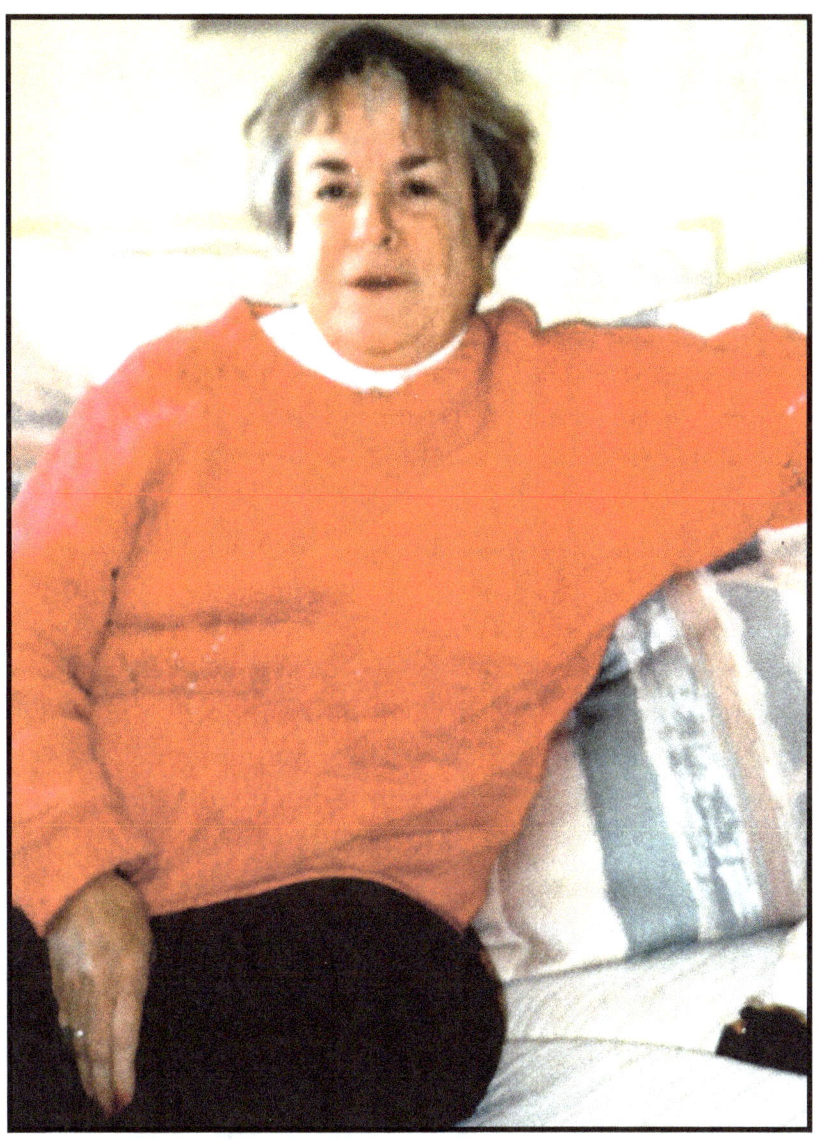

Anne relaxes while discussing plans for Tybee.

working in it and to hear people saying those 30 years were nothing! It's not true."

"What's happening is the deterioration of the American family, and they're using the school system as a scapegoat."

During her first years in administration Anne was breaking ground for women since most principals from Virginia northward were males at that time.

Her success was reflected by the fact that she served as principal at almost a dozen schools for more than 30 years.

Anne declines to say when she was married or specify the length of her matrimonial knot, other than to laugh and say: "It's been long enough."

Suffice it to say that she married Jim Monaghan early in her career, and they now have two grown children and eight grandchildren.

Her marriage enabled her to finally acquire a name befitting her Irish heritage. Her maiden name was Merchant, and the name Monaghan (Jim's grandparents also came from Ireland) fits her like a glove.

Anne has a radiant smile akin to the magnetism of the Blarney Stone.

She admits that, because of her booming voice and precise speech, without that ingratiating smile she might have been quite intimidating to the grade school students who were sent to her office over the years for various infractions.

"I smiled a lot," she says, noting that a key part of her success was "keeping a good sense of humor."

She still remembers the problems caused by one little boy from years past.

"His name was Billy Roper," she laughs. "He had a little beagle dog who followed him to school every day."

"The dog would arrive, and we'd have to call his mother to come pick up the dog. I'd put the beagle in my bathroom. Then the mother would be late coming, and the dog would be howling, and there we were trying to conduct business with a dog howling in the bathroom. Nobody told me it was going to be like that!"

"Those are the things you remember. Your sense of humor keeps you going."

Anne served as principal of four schools in Northern Virginia before taking a similar position in Dayton, Ohio, where she moved with Jim, who was employed as a salesman there.

The two then moved to Louisville, Ky. where they took a turn at entrepreneurship when they established a carpet and interior decorating business.

"We decided to buy a franchise," says Anne.

"I left education and Jim left sales and we decided to try this. We did it for four or five years and it didn't work out as we planned, but we worked together and we were good at it.

"It just didn't pan out the way we wanted."

Following that venture, they returned to the Washington area where Anne again served as a grade-school principal for seven years.

During that time, she and Jim spent much of their off time sailing on nearby Chesapeake Bay aboard "Kumbaya," their 27-foot Pearson sailboat.

They moved to the Savannah area in 1983, after becoming enamored of the area during their travels.

They moved earlier than they originally planned at the urging of Jim's sister, who had purchased property in the area and advised them not to wait until they retired to move down.

"The kids drove our cars and all our stuff down, and all we had left was the cat and our sailboat," says Anne. "We sailed it here. It was a wonderful trip. I can't wait to do it again."

Anne became principal of Charles Ellis School in Savannah, where she and Jim lived for two years before moving to Tybee.

It was considered an inner-city school when she took over, then was turned into a magnet school as the Charles Ellis Montessori Academy, the only public Montessori school in Georgia, during her tenure.

"I really enjoyed the challenge," she says. "I liked it because it fit my philosophy. The Montessori approach reaches children at different levels, and you can walk in a single classroom and have 14 different things going on. It works very well."

She says the major difference she found between schools here and those she administered in Northern Virginia was the lack of technology and the aging school buildings in Savannah.

Major improvements were made in both the programs and the buildings during her 12 years in the school system.

Anne says her current venture into politics was not a spur-of-the-moment decision.

Jim, who is now president of the Tybee Republican Club, ran unsuccessfully for city council just after they moved to the island, and a number of Anne's friends repeatedly suggested that she run for office.

"It was always in the back of my mind," she says, but she waited until after retirement to throw her hat in the ring.

"I found the recent council race kind of fun," she says. "I really enjoyed going around talking to people. I found them most pleasant."

In preparation for taking her seat in January she is putting in long hours studying city operations, especially ordinances and budgets.

There's a lot to learn," she says, "but I enjoy it, and

Anne seems delighted with painting.

I really care about this place. I've put my roots down here and this is home."

She has also spent considerable time meeting with City Manager William Farmer.

"He's great to work with and has given me a lot of time," says Anne. "I've really appreciated it."

Now she's anxious to get started on team building and the preservation of Tybee's appealing appearance.

"I'm interested in how Tybee is going to look," she says.

"I don't want it to look like Anytown, USA. I don't know how we're going to do this, but in between the planning commission and council there needs to be maybe an ARB (Architectural Review Board)."

"The planning commission makes sure everybody complies with the ordinances and council keeps a tight rein on what's happening but somebody needs to ask, 'How do we think it looks' when reviewing building plans."

"I really feel we have to do it because there are a lot of people that build and stay here and love this place, but there are those who build and leave and that's it."

"So far, Tybee's doing all right. We can't stop the growth, but we have to control it. That's uppermost in my mind."

"I want to preserve and project a certain beauty from the Lazaretto Creek Bridge on."

Anne believes the city can work with builders to help them make structures attractive and suggests that what would otherwise be unattractive buildings, such as the storage shed complex now being erected on U.S. 80, could be adorned with paintings, and improved with landscaping.

"That's the reason for a team on council," she says.

"You've got to feed off each other's ideas. You're not there just to bicker with each other. You have one point of view, and I have another, and compromises can be reached. But this bickering and not getting anywhere doesn't do it."

Males may dominate Tybee's council in numbers, but you can bet Anne Monaghan's booming voice will be heard, and her bright smile will light up City Hall.

POSTSCRIPT: Anne Merchant Monaghan served on Tybee City Council for four years. She paved the way for a growing number of women to win seats on that body and ultimately, the election of Shirley Sessions, the island's first female mayor. Anne was 75 when she passed away on June 5, 2010.

Bill Inglis -
Islander Is a Man of Many Means

Engineer Danced on Broadway

*N*eed a choreographer, a tap dancer or perhaps a ballet dancer, all with extensive stage and television experience, or maybe a teacher of these skills?

Or perhaps, given the recent Olympic mania here, you might need a gymnastics instructor or an expert in setting up racecourses for sailing venues?

You can find them all in one man on Tybee Island.

And that's less than half the professional life and skills exhibited by Bill Inglis. He's also had a 29-year career as an electrical engineer.

Of that second career, Bill says he recalls that at age seven, when his elders asked what he wanted to be when he grew up, he quickly replied "an electrical engineer."

"What I meant at age seven was that I wanted to be the driver of one of those electric trains," he chuckles.

***Bill takes a break in Scotland during trip
to check on his ancestry.***

When he became an electrical engineer later in life, it was more happenstance than prophetic.

Despite his many accomplishments, Bill is best known to his island drinking companions as "One Beer Bill."

They claim that he never has more than one beer prior to leaving a lounge but then he moves to another and another while still limiting himself to a single brew in each.

Bill acknowledges the moniker but denies constantly imbibing during his barhopping.

"I really have only one beer... that's all," he claims. "I'm not a drinker."

It's easy to accept Bill's version, given his trim, athletic body and the thick shock of white hair crowning his unlined, tanned face which could easily pass for someone far younger than his age of 68.

His shirt was still drenched in perspiration after mowing the expansive lawn behind his 15th Street house on a torrid Tybee afternoon in August when we chatted with him.

Days earlier, he completed three weeks of hauling in and tossing out buoys for course markers during the Olympic sailing races off Tybee.

Bill was part of the Olympic team on Mark Boat One, the unit charged with setting up the weather mark and the course each day for Soling and Tornado class sailboats.

His efforts entailed strenuous 12-hour days and came on the heels of three years doing similar work for the preparatory races leading up to the Olympics.

Save for the change in hair color, Bill looks little different than he did in publicity photos when he was a dancing star 40 years ago, pictures in which he looked more like a bantamweight boxer than a ballet dancer. If you're seriously looking for one of the talents referred to earlier, Bill might be interested. Given the right opportunity, he says he'd like to become active again in his earlier vocations.

Having studied and performed with the American Ballet Theatre and the New York City Ballet, appeared in numerous popular Broadway musicals and a virtual Who's Who of early television shows, he has impeccable credentials.

He's also directed and choreographed a number of musical productions.

Bill started dancing in Philadelphia when his mother enrolled him in tap-dancing classes at the age of five. At ten, he attended classes at the Littlefield School of Ballet.

By then he had already danced before vintage television cameras in the fledgling medium's experimental days back in 1937.

Bill danced with two girls before stationary cameras for Philco when that company was attempting to capture movement and eliminate "persistence" (the white streak that followed movement across the screen at that time).

He continued his ballet lessons while attending Friends Select School in Philadelphia, a historic Quaker institution chartered in 1689.

Bill plans to attend the 50th anniversary of his graduating class later this year.

After completing high school, he worked briefly as a secretary for an insurance company, while freelancing in his spare time as a dancer on television.

He also worked with the USO throughout World War II, performing in a tap-dancing act in clubs along the East Coast.

Bill quickly learned he was not cut out for insurance work and, at age 20, he headed for New York to pursue a dancing career.

Bill and George Anne Inglis at their home on Tybee.

"I starved for about six months and then got my first job in a Broadway show in 1949," he says.

The musical, *Arms and the Girl* written by Morton Gould, starred Pearl Bailey and John Conte.

Then he joined the American Ballet Theatre on tours of Europe, South America, Canada, and all of the then 48 U.S. states.

Later, he worked with George Balanchine in the New York City Ballet while also doing modern, jazz-type "show dancing" in Broadway musicals and early TV shows.

Among his Broadway credits were *Call Me Madam, Kiss Me Kate, Brigadoon, Two's Company, Carousel, Three Penny Opera, Merry Widow* and *Take Me Along.*

"One of the most fun shows I ever did was *Two's Company,*" he says, noting that this was the only Broadway production Bette Davis was ever in and "she was stewed for most of the show's two-month run."

His television appearances included the *Milton Berle Show,* the *Martha Raye Show,* the *Patti Page Show, Voice of Firestone* and the *Pat Boone, Dave King* and *Ed Sullivan* shows, in addition to numerous "television spectaculars."

During the 1970s, Bill was a choreographer and director for musicals, including *Fiddler on the Roof, Promises, Promises, Anything Goes, Zorba, The Most Happy*

Bill beside wall of memorabeilia from dancing days.

Fella, Sugar, A Funny Thing Happened on The Way to The Forum, Brigadoon and the ballet *L'Histoire Du Soldat.*

"I was never really out of work once I got started," he says, noting that he gained a reputation as a quick study and a good dancer.

His last performance in New York was *Take Me Along,* starring Jackie Gleason. By that time Bill said television was changing, with the old live performances and the fun and challenge of having "only one chance to get it right" coming to a close.

He says one of the most exciting - and sometimes amusing - aspects of live TV was the frenzied activity "which frequently included having to change costumes just back of the cameras, while still on stage in front of a live audience."

"This occasionally caused the unaccounted for laughter during the shows. We were mooning the audience!" TV employment opportunities slowed for Bill with the advent of videotaping and canned laughter and a reduction in the number of new musicals on Broadway.

Fortunately, Bill had seen those changes coming and while performing in his last regular television series, *The Pat Boone Show* in 1960, he enrolled in an engineering course at Columbia University.

Boone, incidentally, was enrolled in Columbia at the same time, studying for a degree in theology.

Having married his first wife, who he met while they were both with the New York City Ballet performing in *Call Me Madam,* and now having a child, Bill felt compelled to find more reliable employment and applied for work with Western Electric, the predecessor of Bell Telephone and AT&T, in New Jersey.

He says he was delighted and surprised that the company hired him and paid for his final two years of college to complete his degree as an electrical engineer.

While with the company from 1960 until his retirement in 1989, he purchased a home in Westfield, N.J., and built an addition for a dance studio in which he and his wife taught ballet and ballroom dancing in the evening.

Bill also taught tap dancing and modern jazz and joined his wife performing in area theaters where he served as director and choreographer for a number of productions.

During the late 1970s, he worked at a nearby gym in his spare time teaching ballet and helping young female gymnasts perfect their floor routines.

"That was fantastic," he says. "Those little girls would spend five hours a day working on their routines. Their mothers would drop them off with their lunches. They were great! That was a lot of fun."

Bill's first visit to Tybee came in 1975 when he and his wife decided to make a side trip from their usual vacation spot beside Hartwell Lake just north of Augusta.

They were immediately smitten with the island and, after a second visit the following year, purchased the house where they now reside.

"One Beer Bill" beside Georgianne Inn sign he salvaged.

Bill figures it was fate in more ways than one, that brought him to Tybee. On that second visit to the island, he stayed at the Georgianne Inn on Butler Ave.

Two years after the demise of his first marriage, Bill married George Anne (much like the name of the inn) and they moved to Tybee permanently when he retired in 1989.

Both were delighted recently when they were able to obtain the old Georgianne Inn sign which is now leaning against a wall on their porch until they find the perfect spot to hang it.

George Anne is currently employed with the American Red Cross in Savannah while Bill concentrates on sailing and yard work.

Judging by the wistful look he gets when discussing his former performing days, however, it's easy to imagine he might start a third career any day now.

Better look out Tommy Tune, One Beer Bill may be getting ready for a comeback!

POSTSCRIPT: Bill never quite made that comeback though he remained active working for a while as a radio disc jockey specializing in classical music. William T. "Bill" Inglis passed away March 22, 2003, in his home on Tybee Island. He was 74.

Edwin Longwater -
Sailing Through the Good Life

Charter Captain Savors Leisure, Good Food

*H*e has the name, the look and the nautical knowledge of his charter captain profession but admits he's still a kid in an adult's body.

Capt. Edwin Longwater, a robust man with longish, graying beard and hair, has been cavorting about Tybee's waters swimming, shrimping, fishing and boating since he was a child, and nothing much has changed.

The captain claims he wouldn't have it any other way.

"Your leisure time is worth so much more than your work time even if your work is like leisure," he says.

Edwin's is, incidentally.

He says he prefers not to have more than two or three charters a month on the Sea Lark, his 60-foot, custom-built St. Augustine trawler. This enables him to pay the bills but still embrace his preferred leisure-time activities.

"I'm just going day to day, and I enjoy the hell out of it," he says. "That counts for a lot. I've never had a bad day" since initiating the charter service under the name Palmetto Coast Charters, Inc., operating out of Lazaretto Creek.

Even when he's not working, he doesn't wander far from the beloved local waters where he crabs, swims and fishes or lolls about his boat reading or creating watercolor paintings for friends, except for an occasional round of golf.

As for the latter, Edwin says he shot in the 70s when he was in high school and still manages to break 80 occasionally, even though he gets in no practice between his infrequent trips round the links.

Not only does he have a seaman's look and name, he's got the perfect companion for his water-bound adventures.

That companion is his buddy Mojo, a chocolate lab with a massive head who loves the water as much as his master does.

Mojo, named for a voodoo good luck charm, swims with, befriends, and is befriended by the dolphins which Edwin frequently ferries tourists out to view.

"Mojo swims with them," he says. "The dolphins in the creek know him and will come up and nudge him as they swim and play with him."

"Most times he rides on the bow of the boat, and dolphins swim up and they'll touch snouts as he leans over. Sometimes he licks their heads or will stick his head in their mouths."

"They like Mojo more than they like most people. Dolphins respond to some people and not to others. Sometimes they'll swim up to the boat and let you

Capt. Edwin Longwater with his dog Mojo.

pet them. They like to be petted under their neck, and if they really like you, they'll roll over and let you rub their bellies. Usually, it's the females that do that."

"And they love good music. I took a French lady out who sang lullabies. She had a beautiful voice, and dolphins would gather around the boat to hear her. My own voice is lousy, and the dolphins don't like it at all."

"They particularly like children and women, but not all of 'em. They don't like everybody."

Mojo, on the other hand, apparently does.

The big Labrador retriever sidles up to all comers, sweeping his big tail in an appreciative arc in response to the back scratch they usually offer, and that works out fine for most folks.

Edwin motors around off-shore and inland waters on either the Sea Lark or his 17-foot Boston Whaler, but Mojo's penchant for nuzzling affectionately has circumscribed his social life.

The two used to hang out nights in Cafe Loco, a small restaurant and bar just a mullet's jump from the Sea Lark's dock on Lazaretto Creek.

"We were welcomed there for a while until Mojo got too friendly with the customers and they banned us from the place," laments Edwin.

But the incident wasn't a major problem for the charter boat captain since he doesn't do much bar hopping anyway.

"They've got this law that says you can't drive after you drink, and in my case if I'm caught doing that, I would lose my captain's license," he says. "I think the law is a bit unfair where it relates to ship captains and airlines pilots. Still, you just have to deal with it."

Edwin says he was delighted to learn of the recent initiation of taxi service on Tybee and believes it should be a major benefit to anyone on the island who imbibes and must then navigate home.

Like Mojo, Edwin gets along with virtually everyone on the water. He's welcomed by shrimp boat operators and yachtsmen as well.

"The shrimpers think the Sea Lark (designated as a yacht but with lines similar to those of a shrimp boat) is a classic yacht, and the yachtsmen think it's a shrimp boat," he smiles. "I sort of fall between two groups, and I get along with all of 'em."

Kinship with the sea runs strong in Edwin's family.

His older brother once cruised through area waters in a bateau and used his boat as a beach lifeguard's rescue craft, while his sister is a fish net maker in Fernandina Beach, Fla.

Edwin was born and raised on Tybee, and his parents were natives of Savannah.

He attended Jenkins High School in Savannah, then graduated from Armstrong College with degrees in history and education, later doing graduate work at Savannah State University where he taught classes for a while.

Edwin aboard his trawler the Sea Lark.

But his study never really stopped.

He continued to take a variety of postgraduate courses for 15 years, reads extensively in the fields of history and ecology, and some acquaintances consider him to be both a historian and a naturalist.

Edwin tried joining the corporate world for a while, selling toner for copying machines, but gave that up after a couple of years when he discovered he was not going to get rich and retire within the five years he had projected before starting that venture.

He also joined his father in the construction business and worked closely with plumbing, electrical, carpentry and other subcontractors for several years.

"I learned enough about a lot of things to be dangerous," he laughs.

That experience, in addition to later exposure to marine repairs while employed with a local shipyard, has proved valuable in his current vocation.

The Sea Lark, one of only three St. Augustine trawlers constructed in the early 1960s, was a virtual derelict, listing precariously beside a Lazaretto Creek dock when Edwin first spotted her.

Acquiring the craft fulfilled his life-long ambition to own a big boat but resulted in months of arduous work repairing her hull and almost everything else from stem to stern.

"I learned about big boats and seamanship through on-the-job training, from the bottom up," he laughs. "I never had anything but plastic (boats) before and it's been a real education."

He says he is particularly grateful that there are numerous wooden boat enthusiasts living in this area who have worked with him to supplement his knowledge.

And while the job now seems complete, with the Sea Lark riding high and proudly sporting a new coat of paint, Edwin says both his education and his work may never end.

"That's symptomatic of wooden boats," he says philosophically. "I look forward to another 20 years of it."

And while he does most of the maintenance himself, his predilection is not inexpensive.

"You know what BOAT stands for, don't you?" he grins. "Bring Out Another Thousand dollars."

He says his charters continue to cover the cost and enable him to live, though he's not living especially high on the hog.

"The living is marginal, but the food is magnificent," says Edwin, who specializes in preparing gourmet Low Country cuisine for himself and those who charter his vessel.

He says he continues to read extensively and to learn, through experience, more about seamanship and the myriad complexities of ship operation and maintenance.

While constantly expanding his knowledge, admirers say he is now one of the most knowledgeable people hereabouts concerning coastal and inland waterways from Fernandina Beach, Fla. to Charleston, S.C.

Edwin's first charter craft was a 13-foot Boston Whaler. That grew to a 17-footer, which he named the Barry Jo, and finally to the Sea Lark.

He kept the Barry Jo and tows it along on excursions to ferry folks ashore to explore uninhabited islands and for day trips around inland waters for fishing and dolphin viewing.

Below decks, the Sea Lark features three staterooms, each stocked with numerous books for the pleasure and edification of passengers.

There is also a full galley and salon, while outside there are three decks at different levels and a swim platform.

"Bubba," a stone gargoyle sporting sunglasses and a baseball cap, is a permanent fixture on the rear deck.

Edwin purchased the gargoyle as a gift for his sister, but "she said she hated it," and the friend she was with at the time refused to put it in his car.

Bubba, who the captain has grown quite fond of, has remained on the deck since that time. Edwin claims it keeps bad spirits away.

With a pair of 900-gallon fuel tanks, the Sea Lark has the range for extended blue water cruises, and Edwin says he has toured the Caribbean and is currently considering a cruise to the Bahamas.

One of the unique features of his charter boat is that the upper deck is designed to capture rainwater and funnel it into holding tanks, making it ideal for long voyages.

His charter trips, one-to-five-day excursions for up to six passengers, are generally conducted in the area around Georgia's coastal barrier islands.

Passengers are treated to dolphin viewing, hiking on secluded beaches, shelling, bird watching, exploring creeks and marshes, crabbing, casting for shrimp and mullet, in-shore fishing and relaxing on deck, in addition to consuming copious portions of his delicious food.

On one recent charter, Edwin says he took an avid kayaker to several spots on the coast to enjoy his sport in solitude.

In addition to kayaking through local waters, where the man said the kayaking was the best he has ever experienced, "we swam, sunbathed, ate great food, and enjoyed some delicious wine," recalls Edwin.

Edwin says he continues to enjoy the same "uninterrupted pleasure" as area natives did back in the 1700's.

"Then we sat on deck at night and watched a huge meteor shower. They were everywhere. It just doesn't get any better than that."

That kayak enthusiast apparently agreed. He left his one-man craft aboard the Sea Lark and has already booked three future excursions.

Edwin prefers cruising and living in the Tybee area because of its salt marsh wetlands and six-to-10-foot tidal range.

"Georgia has the largest expanse of salt marsh is the most productive food producing area on earth," he says.

"I only think of going further south when it gets cold here. I love the blue water and snorkeling in the Caribbean, but they don't have the salt marsh or the tides we have. I wouldn't want to be around there very long. I love Tybee."

"A lot of people look at the tides as a detriment, but all of life in this area is based on the tides. Every charter I go out on I have to consider the tides. The birds have to consider them just like the fish and the dolphins. Everyone living in this vicinity lives by the tides."

Edwin figures most people have "dreamed of cruising to the sandy beaches of an uninhabited island somewhere in paradise where the only footprints to be found are those of birds, wild animals or your own."

"Well, paradise is nearby! King George of England had it right when he said Georgia's barrier islands were his Crown Jewels."

"They're the last stretch of wilderness on the east coast. They're simply gorgeous. And you have most of the salt marsh on the east coast of North America right down the 100 miles of Georgia coast. It's pristine!"

Edwin is fond of quoting naturalist William Bartram's observation during his travels through this area in the 1700s when he said natives living in coastal Georgia have "a fullness of pleasure uninterrupted."

Latter day native Capt. Edwin Longwater, who still meanders through these waters just as he did as a boy, seems to personify that lifestyle.

POSTSCRIPT: Edwin Longwater says he has retired from his laid-back lifestyle as a boat captain but continues to live aboard the Sea Lark and is now an ordained minister operating a company called Coastal Weddings the web site for which claims: "I'm just a dinghy ride away from performing your wedding ceremony in the midst of paradise." Mojo is no longer with him, having passed away at age 12 shortly after fathering 11 chocolate labs with another lab named Savannah, who Edwin says he saved from euthanasia at the pound. Mojo "danced around like a pup" when he met Savannah, and "stood in awe watching her deliver their pups," says Edwin. "He died a very happy father" and was buried in the dunes of Little Tybee Island "which have since washed away. He's once again swimming with the dolphins."

Denise Elliot-Vernon -
Poetry and Art: Idyllic Companions

Differences Seem to Bring Them Together

They met when she crashed a party at a Tybee city councilman's house, fell in love in a home built to simulate a sailing ship, and married under a leafless old tree on an uninhabited island.

Now they've started an expanding family although he's in his late 60s, 40 years her senior.

Richard Vernon and Denise Elliot-Vernon are not what you'd call your run-of-the-mill couple.

In addition to other incongruities, Dick is from Sweden and spent much of his life sailing the world at the helm of a ship while Denise was born and reared far from the sea in the mountains of Connecticut.

Dick is a poet who settled on Tybee in 1984 after selling his big Nordic sailboat.

Denise, who is vice president of the Tybee Art Assn., has been an artist since she was in grade school and will have her first art show in Savannah on Jan. 18, featuring at least a dozen of her paintings in both acrylics and watercolors. It will be held for a month in the Savannah Fine Arts Gallery at the corner of Liberty and Bull Streets.

Dick will participate in the show with his poetry. They plan to have him read several of his poems relating to her paintings during the exhibit and will either display his work with her paintings or in a special booklet.

They do most things together, and seem perfectly matched, despite their differences.

Dick was there when Dylan, their 16-month-old son, was born in a tub filled with warm water. Denise is now expecting again and plans to birth their second child, also a boy, in the same manner, with Dick again in attendance.

"The warm water is so relaxing and natural," Denise explains. "It's just a wonderful experience."

The process is said to be an unusually comfortable way for a child to enter the world because it's a natural transition from the warm wetness of the womb into a warm and wet world.

Pictures of Denise during Dylan's birthing, along with an article describing the process at the Family Health and Birth Center in Rincon, Ga., were published in Modern Maturity magazine.

When Dylan was conceived, Dick wrote a poem entitled "Tidebound" to complement Denise's painting of a barren old cedar tree on Little Tybee Island with the same title.

Denise decided that it would be beside this tree that their wedding would take place. A hundred wedding guests were ferried to the uninhabited island to attend the ceremonies.

Denise grew up with four siblings in the little town of Milford, Conn., where she produced pen and ink

Denise and Dick Vernon with painting of Little Tybee tree where they were wed.

drawings for cards and gifts when she was still in grade school.

She claims she got her artistic inclination from her older brother "who did all kinds of artful things like painting and wood burning, anything creative. He's now rebuilding an old barn back home in Connecticut. It'll have living space, a basketball court, a studio, and other stuff. It's huge."

She visits her close-knit family frequently and hopes one day to have a second home in Maine.

Although her roots remain in New England, her shapely branches have blossomed on Tybee, where she plans to remain.

While in high school, Denise worked at an art gallery where she displayed her paintings and sold her first one before she graduated. The painting featured pigs lined up along a trough. It sold for $125.

"I sold or gave away everything I painted," she recalls. "There was never a question that I would be anything else but an artist."

There was a question about where she should attend college to hone her craft, however. She looked at schools in New York and California before coming to Savannah to inspect the facilities at the Savannah College of Art and Design, better known as SCAD.

"It's just fantastic," she says. "When I came down with my mother, I knew in two seconds that this was where I should be. It had so much space. The architecture and the classroom space are great, and there's so much light, and it has this wonderful spiral staircase."

"I couldn't stand it in New York. Rooms were cramped little spaces. It was claustrophobic. And I hated California. It's too materialistic. People were worried about fashions and the cars they drove. The prices were very high, and the traffic was incredible."

For her junior year, Denise did attend an art school in Los Angeles but that simply reaffirmed her disdain for the West Coast. She even tried spending a year in northern California, thinking that maybe it was just the southern part of the state she disliked.

It wasn't.

Denise then returned to her home in Connecticut for six months, spending that time working at several jobs to earn enough money to return to Savannah, where she was finally able to graduate from SCAD.

Along the way, she fell in love with Tybee, driving out whenever she could.

She usually made the trip at night so she could swim in the ocean by moonlight and marvel at the phosphorescence trailing behind her.

Denise met Dick at a party at the home of Tybee Councilman Mallory Pearce.

Denise discusses her art.

"We crashed that party," she says, recalling that she came with Angela Beasley, a friend with whom she had performed puppet shows for several years.

"We brought our puppets, and we were the life of the party," she says, noting that Mallory has a particular affinity for puppets since his mother once worked as a puppeteer.

Dick made an immediate impression on the young artist.

"He had this wonderful flowing hair, and he was tall and just so self-confident," says Denise. "I saw him right away, and he pulled up a chair and cornered me."

Even though she was impressed, she figured nothing much would come of it.

"I had just broken up with my boyfriend the day before and I wasn't feeling very sociable," she recalls. "I didn't even want to go to that party."

Neither Dick nor Denise tried getting in touch after the party, but several months later they met by happenstance at Tybee's Marlin Marina, and Dick invited her to his house for a smorgasbord dinner he was hosting for several friends.

After the other guests departed, "Dick talked to me for hours, telling me everything about himself, just pouring it out," smiles Denise. "I never met anyone so honest or so sure of himself. I found that most attractive. I was so tired of the games the little boys I had been dating played."

Dick, who had been married three times previously, described those relationships along with everything else.

"His first wife was a model," says Denise. "She was beautiful. They were all beautiful women. I was a little intimidated."

"Then Dick told me that if we were going to see each other, it had to be just him. He wasn't going to have me seeing anybody else."

"I said well, I guess I'll just have to break up with my boyfriend," and she did just that.

She says the breakup wasn't a big problem because she was dating a guy in show business who used to "blow himself up, inflate himself, and then entertain by doing gymnastics and stuff. Hey, I figured he was full of hot air anyway."

Dick designed and built their house, an unusual structure full of windows, curved decks, and angles, that overlooks Horsepen Creek and the marsh beyond.

The house looks and feels like a sailing ship, which is exactly what Dick had in mind.

"You stand on the balcony and it's like being on the deck of a ship ready to sail off over the marsh," he says, gazing westward, arms akimbo, looking for all the world like the tall, trim sea captain of yore.

Everything about the house is airy, even the bathroom, which has no door.

"That does cause some of our guests to get a little uncomfortable," observes Denise, "but we like it."

The creek and marsh have been inspirational for Denise, who has done a number of paintings of the dolphins that swim past her studio, which sits atop their dock.

She captures a variety of moods with those dolphins. Some signify motion, others almost motionless tranquility.

Denise has also done several paintings of wave-worn seashells she gathers on the beach, most having a distinctly erotic quality reminiscent of Georgia O'Keeffe's flowers.

In addition to her forthcoming exhibit, Denise is rekindling her interest in puppets and plans to write the skits and plays in which they will be used.

Ultimately, she hopes to obtain a grant for puppet performances featuring "environmental characters" for shows on Tybee and in Savannah and the surrounding area, principally for children and senior citizens.

"The idea would be to teach the kids about plants, flora and fauna, and things like that," she says.

Dick, whose work has been published in several poetry magazines, stays busy writing short stories, essays, and poetry, much of which is associated with Denise's paintings.

He's also giving serious thought to writing an autobiography, which should be quite a read.

Dick was born in Sweden and at age 18 he started working on tramp steamers and tall ships sailing around the Horn of Africa.

After becoming an Able-Bodied Seaman, he served in the Royal Swedish Navy for two years aboard mine-

Denise stands beside one of her dolphin paintings.

sweepers, then worked on merchant vessels for a couple of years before coming to the United States where he joined the Marine Corps during the Korean War.

Dick studied aeronautical engineering in night school, then worked for the Grumman Corp. for eight years before sailing up and down the East Coast for a while on his 28-foot sloop.

He and his first wife, Ulla, sailed to the Virgin Islands where they worked in the charter fleet for nine years before purchasing the Nordic, a big yawl on which they lived.

Dick says Ulla served as first mate on the ship that he claims was the largest fiberglass and epoxy sailing vessel in the world at that time.

After becoming a master mariner, he says he hosted numerous government and industry leaders on charters, and that Walter Cronkite and Jason Robards were among his sailing companions.

When Ulla passed away, Dick sold the Nordic to a company which retained him to convert the yawl into a research vessel.

He still savors his memories of the sea, which is apparent in the opening lines of his poem, "Lament of a Landbound Sailor":

> *"I miss the sea spray upon my lips,*
> *the smells the trade winds carried;*
> *I miss the drive, the swells of seas*
> *with which the wind was married."*

Meanwhile, Denise still dreams of that second home on the craggy coast of Maine.

Although their dreams seem diverse, you might travel many a windswept coast or sail over untold seas before you could find a closer or more creative couple.

POSTSCRIPT: *Richard Vernon passed away not long after this was written. Denise took two-year hiatus from painting, before returning to her craft and conducting art classes for adults. She*

has served as president of the Tybee Arts Association, staged a number of successful exhibits, and remains among the most popular artists in the area.

Edmund Solomon -

Long Time Resident Savors Memories

Beach Was
The Place
To Be

*E*yes twinkling, Edmund J. Solomon remembers Tybee's halcyon days when you could dance until the early hours summer nights on the old Tybrisa Pavilion, then curl up beneath it and doze until dawn, dash into the surf for a refreshing morning dip, and frolic on the beach all day before doing it all over again.

Edmund, now 84 and a respected fixture on the island, did it all, dancing to Dorsey's big band and sleeping with friends on the beach, knowing his parents never worried because, he smiles, "What could go wrong on Tybee?"

When he wasn't basking or dozing on the beach, Edmund was usually fishing and crabbing in a leaky wooden boat on the Back River.

"You could rent a boat with long oars for a buck, and it would hold five people," he recalls.

Those rowboats were rented at Tybee Boats, where
Marlin Marina is now located.

"We called 'em Tybee's Leaking Boats 'cause they
leaked like a sieve," he laughs. "You had to carry two
big buckets along, one to keep bailing the things out
and another, filled with cement, to use as an anchor."

"You could get a bushel of crabs in a couple of hours
back then, and the river was crowded with luxury
yachts which came over from the city to bring the
wealthy folks" for outings at the beach.

Edmund moved to Tybee with his family from Isle
of Hope in 1920. His father operated the waterworks
and laid the first water lines on the island. Those water lines are still in place and are now badly in need of
repair, he warns.

Edmund helped his father build the base for the old
water tower on Butler Ave. in 1935, and started the
Edmund Solomon Plumbing Co. That company is
still operated by his son Chris, although he changed
its name to the Tybee Plumbing Co.

While serving as the town's plumbing inspector for
years, Edmund wrote city's first plumbing ordinance
in 1944 and still has a copy of the original ordinance.

These days he spends most of his time carving artistic birds and dolphins and reminiscing in a wood-
working shop crammed full of ancient tools behind
his house on 2nd Ave.

And he still loves to spend summer afternoons fishing on the river when he's not doing maintenance on the several rental properties he and his wife, Dorothy, own.

Dorothy pretty much stays in the main house up front where her husband has assembled an interesting collection of memorabilia, leaving Edmund to his work and memories in the shop out back.

"I got a damned good woman, but I ain't going to tell her that," he says of Dorothy. "You ruin a woman by telling her that."

After his family moved to Tybee, Edmund rode the train to attend Junior High School in Savannah. The ride cost 27 cents.

Pair of tickets to Tybee Island on Central of Georgia Railway. Edmund's son Chris found the tickets after his father passed away.

He finished high school at Georgia Military Academy, then enrolled in North Carolina State University in Raleigh but was forced to drop out and return to the island in 1933 to work with his father because of the Depression.

He assisted his father at the waterworks, on construction of the old Hunter Army Air Base in Savannah and building houses on Tybee. Later, Edmund built a number of Tybee houses on his own.

He says he helped build a large addition to a house at the corner of 7th Street and Butler Avenue which has recently been renovated and is now scheduled to become a bed and breakfast.

"It was a huge place when we finished and it was the only house with a basement on the island," according to Edmund, who says it was located next to the old Atlantic Club Station, the fourth stop on Tybee for the train from Savannah.

Like the handful of other island residents who were here 60 years ago, he has fond memories of the old train bringing crowds of joyous, beach-bound travelers out from the city in open rail cars.

Some news stories claim the train ceased to exist in 1933, a victim of automobiles and the new road to the island, but Edmund remembers the train continued to operate until 1940, delivering material to the Army Diving School on Tybee before it was finally shut down.

The train's roadbed now serves as a bike and hiking path beside Highway 80, just beyond the turnoff to Fort Pulaski.

Edmund can still show you the old cement foundation near the corner of Inlet and Chatham Avenue which served as a turntable for the train at its terminus on Tybee's south end.

"They'd turn the train around there to head it back toward Savannah," he recalls.

After opening his own plumbing company, Edmund married in 1937 and divorced in 1976 after having five

Edmund's extended family gathered for an informal photo. They include, left to right, Edmund's brother Johnny Solomon, his step-mother Blanche Solomon, Edmund Solomon, his granddaughter Maria Solomon-Schafer, his great-grandson Michael Solomon, his wife Frances Solomon, and his grandson Thomas Solomon Jr.

children, three of whom still live on Tybee. He married Dorothy in 1979.

In 1959, he became a founder of Tybee's Marine Rescue Squadron which has aided thousands of boats in distress. The squadron has 30 members now and continues to assist boaters near the island.

Edmund became the city building inspector in 1975, was named plumbing inspector in 1981, and held both positions until his retirement in 1991.

"Those were busy times," with many good days and some "miserable ones," he recalls, noting that the island's elected officials often knew very little about the infrastructure.

Edmund, who worked under five mayors and numerous city councils, says he supports the new city manager system because it makes city operations more businesslike.

In the old days a lot of councilmen had their "old friends who always wanted something," he says.

"We really needed this type of government. I believe in it. I don't know the city manager, but he's got his work cut out for him with all the stuff he's going to find out if he stays long enough."

Edmund says he's a fan of City Councilman Jack Youmans, who has been an elected official on the island for more years than most people can remember.

"He's a man," says Edmund. "He's never been afraid to stand up and say what he thinks."

But Edmund is not happy with some of the changes on the island.

"There are too many dang rules now," he says. "Hell, you can't drop a cigarette ash on the beach without having the law come down on you!"

And he's concerned about the influx of new people.

In his youth the island had only about 900 permanent residents, a number that has grown to nearly 3,000.

"A lot of these people moved here because they didn't have enough money to buy on Hilton Head," he says.

Edmund Solomon tells tales of life on Tybee.

"This was a beautiful place and now they want to change this and change that, and they want to run the place."

While he admires the new pier, which officially opened in August, he says after making one trip out on it, he doesn't plan to return.

"There're just too many people out there, too many outsiders," he says. "There's not room enough for locals to fish or do anything."

Still, it conjures sweet memories of the old Tybrisa pavilion and the glory days of the grand hotels on the island, he says, days when he spent the summers of his youth lolling in the sand, savoring the sounds of the music and the surf.

Those are the days he still contemplates while hunkering down in the little shop behind his house.

POSTSCRIPT: Edmund Solomon was 89 when he passed away on July 12, 2002. His ashes were buried beside the old oyster roaster behind his house. His son Chris says his father frequently sat beside that roaster savoring a drink while the oysters were roasting and that he knows his Dad would have liked being there. Edmund's widow, Dorothea Williams Greene Solomon, was 77 when she died on July 3, 2009 in their family home.

Jim Green -

Keeping It Strange on the Island

This Guy Makes Being Different A Work of Art

*H*ang around Tybee long enough and you'll meet a variety of off-center types, typically referred to as "characters."

Then there are those who've taken it a step further. Those are the "odd characters."

Jim Green has meandered even further afield. Not to put too fine a point on it, Jim could be called a "character's character."

Like fishing or craft work is for some, being different is an avocation for Jim. He thrives on shock value and, if you can believe what he says (there are those who caution against this), he's considering making a career of his predilection.

Ask acquaintances about Jim and they'll either laugh uproariously as they recall some antic, or frown and shrug their shoulders in dismay.

So many strange tales have circulated about him that most are ready to accept any anecdote regarding the man, no matter how cockamamie, with the result that much of what is attributed to him may be speculative, uncorroborated rumor, or flat out wrong.

Take that frequently repeated yarn about Jim biting the head off a live pigeon.

"That's not true," he says. "It was a parakeet!"

Besides, it was something that any macho Army Ranger bellying up to the Ft. Bragg NCO Club bar with Jim's mind set and blood alcohol level might have done.

The guy with the parakeet was a real loudmouth who plopped down on a bar stool beside Jim and his Ranger buddies and just kept talking about this bird... how great it was, and how he had just bought it for his wife, and stuff like that.

So, when the annoying big mouth got up to return some of the beer he'd consumed to the ecosystem, leaving his boxed bird behind on the bar, what could have been more normal than for Jim to grab the thing and chomp off its head?

While Jim's buddies were convulsed with laughter, the owner wasn't particularly amused when he returned to find his bird had lost its head.

Jim still doesn't understand why he was so upset, noting that "Heck, once he calmed down, I offered to give him the money to get another one."

Anyway, that was a long time ago, and Jim claims he hasn't done anything so unseemly since.

"Well, there was that thing with the frog," he confesses. "That wasn't that long ago."

Turns out the Chatham County sheriff's wife was sitting there, quite prim in her sweet summer dress, looking on at a baseball game in Tybee's Jaycee Park in Ft. Screven, a game in which Jim happened to be participating.

He walked up to her, leaned over, and coughed a couple of times before the frog hopped out of his mouth and landed in the lady's lap.

She regaled the crowd with high pitched screams while Jim apologized profusely proclaiming: "I'm really sorry. I had a frog in my throat!"

Seems he saw the toad in the grass as he approached the group the sheriff's wife was sitting with and couldn't resist popping it in his mouth and doing his thing to burst the bubble of propriety surrounding the scene.

That's what he does.

Some, not surprisingly, don't cotton to it.

Jim and Nancy, his wife of 32 years, caused a bit of distress for islanders not long ago, during the con-

Jim Green & wife, Nancy.

troversy over the Georgia state flag and the growing pressure to eliminate the Stars & Bars emblazoned on it.

They draped a banner across the deck of their house - which is clearly visible from Highway 80-with a replica of the Georgia state flag alongside one embellished with a Nazi swastika.

"Keep the Georgia flag or they'll pick one for us" was printed in large letters between the two flags.

"We're not racists, or anti-Semitic, or anything like that," says Jim. "The message was that the Nazi flag is a symbol of evil and there's nothing wrong with the Georgia flag. When they start banning flags, you never know what they might come up with."

The Greens agreed to eliminate the banner when word reached them that Tybee's tourism boosters were panicking because television crews were enroute from Savannah to film the flags.

"Besides, we only planned to leave it up for seven days and the time was about up," says Jim.

Then there's the story about the time the decision was made to move the post office from the south end to its present location, directly in front of the Greens' house.

Several islanders swear Jim donned a camouflage suit and armed himself before climbing a tree on the post office property and holding construction workers at bay for days.

"The truth is," says Jim, "we thought they were going to remove all those old trees on the property and Nancy and I decided to chain ourselves to one of them and refuse to let them cut it down."

Ultimately, no chaining was necessary since the government had always intended to save most of the trees, and the Greens have no problem with their post office neighbor.

"It's a nice, quiet operation," observes Jim. "Hey, it could have been a bar or an all-night Burger King."

Such erroneous tales are a burden that evocative, free-spirited folks like Jim must carry.

Sometimes his "stuff" is actually initiated inadvertently.

"The Brotherhood" originated that way.

Jim simply shaved his head to be cool and somewhat different, in the summer of '86.

Then some guy said he liked Jim's head that way and Jim volunteered to make a video of the man if he shaved his own head. Eventually, 17 guys wound up with shaved heads along with official ID cards designating them as members of "The Brotherhood."

Back in 1988, in a slather of concern for Tybee's weal, Jim ran for mayor.

He didn't win, didn't even come close, but he did have fun and his campaign tee shirts were quite popular.

They featured a mayonnaise bottle with the label "Graft" and urged: "Vote for Jim (Mayonnaise) Green for Mayor of Tybee."

In smaller letters were the words: "He doesn't really want to serve the people of Tybee; he just needs the extra money."

The mayonnaise thing (a number of islanders still refer to Jim as "Mayo") stems from one of his songs, *"I Just Want a Girl Who'll Shove Mayonnaise up My Nose."* He sang it in a summer talent contest at the DeSoto Beach Hotel... and won!

Jim says he has written more than 600 songs.

Most are of the same ilk, songs like: *"Hand Me the Hammer Momma, There's a Fly on the Baby's Head"* and *"She Was Coyote Ugly."*

He says he hopes to put some of his more circumspect tunes together in an album one day.

Jim also produces video films and claims he has more than 161 of them.

The videos trend toward the weird as well, of course, unless you don't think having folks shoot down a passing plane, as they do in his *"Video 100"* for disturbing their conversation, is a bit odd ball. (Most viewers are pretty sure the plane really wasn't shot down.)

If his songs don't make it, Jim hopes the videos will add fortune to his fame. He plans to have them played in local bars to amuse the customers, many of whom are in the films, figuring the shows should at least encourage them to drink more.

He has already had some success marketing in island bars.

Jim created "Iguana Beer" back in 1991 and convinced several Tybee bar owners to carry his product, which sold for $5 a bottle.

He produced 200 bottles and claims every one was purchased, though he suspects most folks bought "or swiped" the beer as a collector's item because those who actually drank it said, "the stuff tasted like pig crap."

"It was just Tybee water in colored beer bottles with an Iguana label," he says, though some speculate that there could be ingredients in the island's water which Jim himself is unaware of.

He also gained some dubious fame in a "battle of the pens" with a former Tybee bar owner. The "battle" consisted of Letters to the Editor columns in Savannah's newspaper.

Jim says he differed, philosophically, with Tom Burns who was critical of 16th Street activities, claiming there were prostitution and drug problems on Tybee, and was pressing to "clean it up and turn it into something it wasn't."

Jim sided with a Tybee City Councilman Jack Youmans who claimed the prostitution allegation was ridiculous since "You can't have prostitution when you can get all you want on this island for free."

Jim created the "Let's get Tom Burns off the Island Committee" and had himself elected as president. Then he painted a sign on a 4 by 8-foot sheet of plywood and placed it at the Lazaretto Creek Bridge for everyone departing the island to read.

"If you're heading north, please take Tom Burns with you," the sign read.

Burns later left the island,

On reflection, Jim now says Burns "really had some good ideas. He just had a lousy way of presenting them. I never had anything against the man. I never even met him."

Jim was once considered something of a news media mogul himself. He wrote, edited, and published the *16th St. Gazette*, in 1991.

"I started it as a joke for a few friends, but people started copying it, and the demand just kept growing," he recalls.

The newspaper lasted for only four editions but increased in size from four pages to twelve at its height, while stirring both chuckles and controversy on the island.

The *Gazette* quoted then Tybee Mayor George Hosti with telling a Savannah newspaper reporter: "I don't like that kind of paper at all. 16th Street has a bad enough reputation without something like this."

Most of the *Gazette*'s material consisted of dark humor, much of it unprintable here or in any other relatively respectable publication.

That part of the publication's masthead disclaimer which can be printed in a family newspaper said the *Gazette* "is published whenever we damn well feel like it" and may not "be reproduced in any manner without explicit written permission from Pharaoh's Witch Doctor. This publication is based on lies, white lies and half-truths. We cannot vouch for the ethical or moral character of anyone whose name appears herein."

Circulation was claimed to be 10,000, although one suspect's that may be one of those half-truths.

Truth be told, Jim hasn't devoted his entire life to such fun and frivolity.

Most of his penchant for such stuff surfaced only after he and Nancy moved to Tybee ten years ago, which may finally put to rest claims that the island's water and breeze promote good mental health, among other things.

Jim was born and reared in Richmond, Va. and attended Miller Military Academy in Charlottesville, Va., prior to joining the Army in 1964, the same year he married Nancy, a former childhood playmate.

His military career, much of it deadly serious, lasted 20 years.

Jim served with E Company, 75th Rangers in Vietnam and was awarded a Purple Heart, three Air Medals and four Bronze Stars for heroism.

His service assignments included the infantry, military intelligence, public affairs and recruiting. In the latter position Jim was once honored as the Army's top recruiter for the year.

He was also a commentator on military radio and television broadcasts while stationed at Ft. Stewart and Hunter Army Air Base prior to his retirement as first sergeant for a 310-man company.

Just after enrolling in jump school early in his career, Jim says he thought he might get a cushy position as a military jock after winning the battalion's heavy-weight boxing championship but when he tried out

Jim Green has a different view of things.

for "the real, full-time boxing team" at Ft. Campbell "I got beat so bad in the tryouts, I learned the infantry was better than boxing."

Not long ago he started a house painting company since "no one shoots at painters" and painting beats being shot at.

That observation stems from his discovery that people sometimes shoot at folks who try to repossess their vehicles.

He learned that lesson the hard way while working as a "Midnight Repo Man" in the Savannah area for four years.

Jim says he repossessed 1,300 vehicles, was shot at nine times, and was arrested twice for snatching vehicles in states where his company had no jurisdiction.

It was after the arrests and finding that his friends names sometimes appeared on repo lists ("I refused to go after anyone I knew," he says) that Jim decided to cease ducking and join the law,

He became a corrections officer at the Chatham County Jail.

"I really liked that work, particularly on the mental ward, " he says.

But he gave that job up on principal when his son, charged with two minor infractions involving bad checks, turned himself in and authorities refused to arrest the boy because of Jim's position.

"They told him to go home and come back with the money to cover the checks," says Jim.

"When I said he needed to learn his lesson and should be treated like everyone else, they said it would be too dangerous for him in jail if other prisoners learned that he was the son of a corrections officer."

"I loved that job, but I just had to quit."

His wife Nancy had a highly successful career of her own in law enforcement.

She was initially hired as a security guard at Oglethorpe Mall, then rose through the ranks to sergeant and lieutenant before leaving that position to become a dispatcher with the Tybee Police Department.

Nancy was lured back to the mall's security force when she was offered a job as chief of security, a position she held for two years before retiring.

Now she claims she's just a housewife who's spending some time thinking about "what I really want to be when I grow up."

Both seem to have given up on that ever happening to Jim.

POSTSCRIPT: *Jim and Nancy Green sold their house behind the post office and moved to Met-*

ter, Ga., not long after this was written where they seem to be keeping a low profile. Folks say it's been years since they were last seen on Tybee. Such characters are fast disappearing from the island, leaving a void in what was once its funkier side.

Helen Curtis -
A Curious and Circuitous Route

Artic Adventure
Ends at
The Beach

*E*ver think about hunkering down on the edge of the Arctic Circle in a village only accessible by plane, and even then, only occasionally, when weather permits?

Few residents of our balmy Georgia islands do, but Helen Curtis not only thought about it, she did it, living in Canada for 21 years, 10 of them near the North Pole.

And she loved it!

"Those were the best 21 years of my life!" she recalls. "I love Tybee, but life in Canada's Northwest Territory was the best I have had."

But don't think she's simply reflecting on the youthful exuberance of her early years. Helen, now approaching 85, set out for the remote area when she was in her late 50s.

It all started somewhat serendipitously when she and her second husband, Fred, went on a camping trip in 1971 to get their priorities in order after Fred resigned his position as supervisor of public works in Calais, Maine.

"It was May and we decided to head north into Canada," according to Helen.

"When we came to a crossroad where you could turn either left or right, we went left, since we were already familiar with Newfoundland and Nova Scotia."

It was a glorious trip, says Helen, remembering the day they came upon a huge field filled with snow geese migrating north.

"The entire area was white with snow geese," she says, still marveling at the memory. "There were thousands and thousands of them!"

Helen and Fred frequently found the campgrounds where they stayed were also white, since they were usually covered with snow.

Along the way, they decided they would push on to see the west coast of Canada.

When they reached Alberta and the base of the Rockies, they came to another road and another choice. They could either continue over the Rockies to British Columbia or turn right towards northern Canada.

"We just decided to turn right and go as far north as the road would carry us," says Helen.

They wound up in a small town called Yellowknife, the capitol of the Northwest Territories, on the north shore of Great Slave Lake, but that wasn't as far north as their travels would ultimately take them.

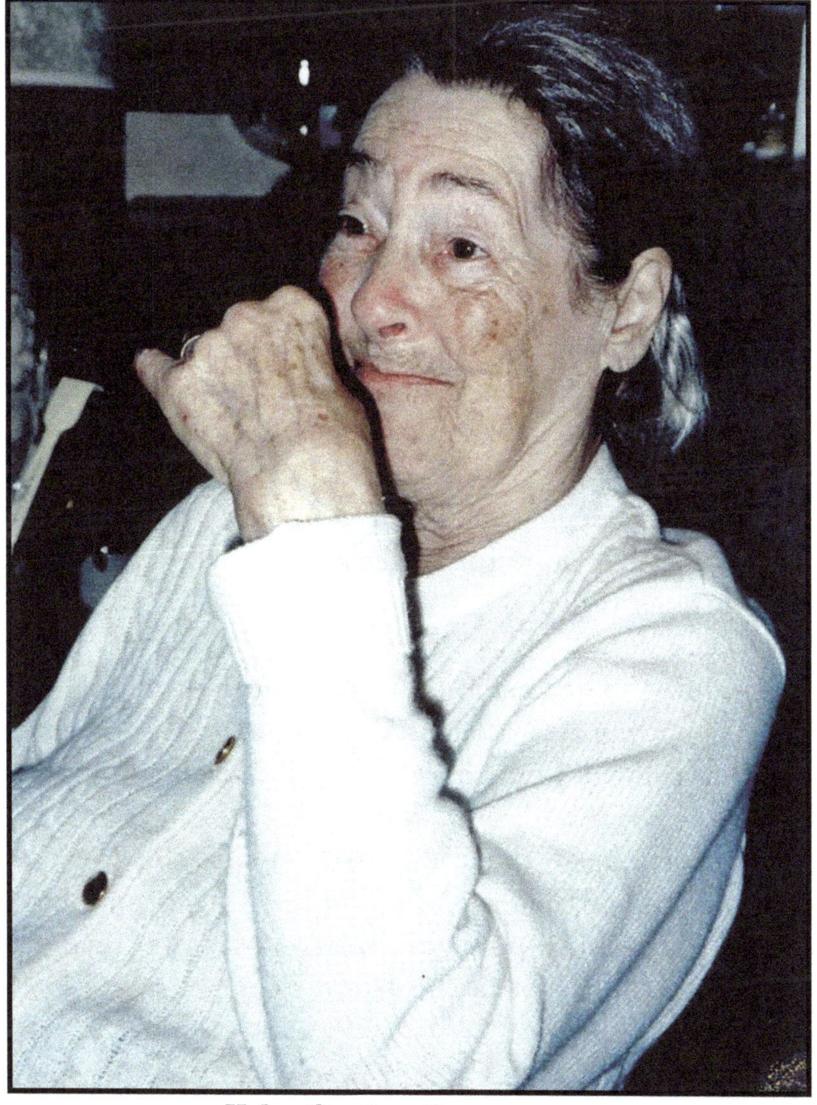

Helen Curtis reflects on past.

While camping beside the lake through the summer, local residents, including government officials, visited them and, learning of Fred's background in construction with public works in Maine, urged him to join the Northwest Territories Public Works Department as a construction supervisor for its dam, highway and airport building program.

Fred agreed, which led to their extended stay in northern Canada.

Much of his time was spent in Snowdrift, a remote settlement 90 miles from Yellowknife on Great Slave Lake.

Fred's assignment was to help plan and build an airport so residents there could have contact with the outside world year-round.

Without the airport, planes had to land on the lake and could only do so in winter months when the ice was sufficiently thick.

Helen joined her husband intermittently in Snowdrift, spending two months there and then a month back in Yellowknife, where they purchased a house.

The house, one of the first constructed in the area, was situated at the base of "The Rock," a prominent landmark for bush pilots around Yellowknife since it was the highest spot in the area.

The small cottage on their property was actually anchored to The Rock.

"I guess you could say I literally owned a piece of The Rock," Helen laughs.

She frequently entertained local Inuits (formerly called Eskimos, a Native American term meaning "raw meat eater, netter of snowshoes" or "speaker of a foreign language," but abandoned when many found the name offensive).

After having met Helen and Fred in Snowdrift, the Inuits frequently showed up at their house when they ventured into Yellowknife.

One of the young men always left his money with Helen when he came into town.

"He knew that if he kept the money it would likely be gone after one night at the nearest bar," she explains.

In addition to Yellowknife and Snowdrift, the couple also spent a lot of time at even more remote villages on the north end of Baffin Island in the Arctic Ocean, which is only a hearty snowball's throw from the North Pole.

They spent an entire summer 700 miles south of the Pole, during which time they made a brief visit to Grise Fiord, the northernmost settlement in North America.

Helen harbors fond memories of the extended summer daylight hours in northern Canada, where full darkness sometimes never came, and she revels in recollections of the midnight sunsets across Great Slave Lake and spectacular aurora borealis light shows.

She recalls one embarrassing moment when members of the village council on Ellesmere Island came to their lodgings to meet with Fred to discuss the construction of a new airport.

Helen and Fred had arrived on the island at 11 p.m., long after the only store in the village had closed and found virtually no provisions in the house they were assigned.

It is customary at such "mugups" with villagers to provide tea and cookies, but Helen had neither tea nor cookies. Instead, she brewed cups of clear broth from bouillon cubes she found in the pantry along with crackers of an indefinable vintage.

"It was terrible, but the villagers were wonderful," she recalls. "They are such a wonderful group of people, the Inuits. They're always smiling."

Helen made a solo excursion down to San Francisco to visit her daughter during that decade. Then she found her return trip to Snowdrift was filled with high adventure.

An airline strike grounded her plane in Seattle so she was bused to Vancouver, B.C., where she was stranded for days.

Frustrated, Helen booked passage on a train to Edmonton, Alberta, obtaining the last available seat for the trip. Fortunately, that last seat consisted of a private, double compartment with a private bath.

"It was quite luxurious, just heavenly," she says. It was, however, a molasses-slow, 24-hour journey because it was the first trial run along recently repaired rail lines which had been damaged by an avalanche.

Helen considered this her good fortune since the slow passage enabled her to gaze out upon spectacular scenery while seated serenely behind the large window in her compartment.

"The mountains were just fabulous," she recalls, noting that she frequently spotted mountain goats grazing in the hills just outside her window.

"And the food they served on the train was absolutely wonderful," she says. "It was the trip of a lifetime!"

Helen's memorable train ride ended at the railroad's Edmonton terminus, from where she planned to fly to Snowdrift.

That plan ended when foul weather grounded all flights.

After a lengthy delay, Helen discovered a bus that was bound for Yellowknife and climbed aboard.

"It was one of the old buses that had been taken out of service in a more populous area and relegated to this remote passage," she says.

The bus labored along perilous roads until it reached the shore of Great Slave Lake long after dark.

That's where the ancient vehicle's generator failed, leaving the bus with no lights and no heat.

Knowing his passengers would not survive an extended stay on the shore, the driver told all aboard to crowd together for warmth and, by the light of the moon, they proceeded across the frozen lake by foot to Yellowknife.

Once reaching Yellowknife, Helen hitched a ride aboard a small Royal Canadian Mounted Police plane to Snowdrift where she was finally reunited with Fred.

Helen remembers a mammoth iceberg floating majestically back and forth with the tides just off the High Arctic village in which they stayed on Baffin Island.

"Oh, it was just beautiful," she says.

During their extended visits to the village, Helen says she was corralled into the role of chief cook, bottle washer and laundress for the seven men who were working with Fred on the airport project.

"They had no time to come in and prepare their meals or wash their clothes, so that became my job in addition to being the cook and Mother Confessor to the group," smiles Helen.

That was not the first job she had stumbled into, although the earlier ones at least carried a salary.

Helen, who was born and reared in Boston, attended a series of private boarding schools in and around the city.

One of those upscale institutions, Curtis Peabody School on Boston's Beacon Street, started an innovative "outdoor school" featuring classes on the lawn for the younger girls.

"I remember we sat around outside in the winter tucked in sleeping bags up to our waists," says Helen.

Then, there was the year she rode her horse, Prince, seven-and-a-half miles to class each day at Miss Allen's School in West Newton, Mass.

Helen claims she led a very sheltered life through high school.

"I don't recall ever having any freedom," she says, noting that she had only one "arranged" date for her senior "tea dance" at Miss Allen's School.

Even though socially sheltered, she was already a woman of the world however, having traveled to Europe three times in 1925, 1927 and 1929.

She received her international driver's license when she was still 15, just before departing for the 1929 trip.

While still a novice, Helen drove a Ford touring car

along a treacherous route over the Pyrenees mountains on that trip.

"I knew so little about cars that I was unaware I
should down shift to reduce speed while heading
down those steep mountain roads," she says. "I rode
the brakes all the way down the far side of the Pyrenees. When I got to the bottom they were completely
gone."

Helen entered Boston University's College of Liberal
Arts five days after she turned 17.

Her family had wanted her to go to Radcliff, but she
felt it was too "blue stocking" and insisted that if she
was going to remain in the area, she would attend the
university.

Helen says her social life remained noticeable for its
absence until her junior year in college.

That was when she met Merrill, who worked in school
administration, and quickly made up for lost time.
They married shortly after she received her degree.

"He wanted to marry me right away, and I was one
of those people who had never made many decisions
for myself," she says. "It was one of those kinds of
things."

Helen busied herself having children and doing extensive volunteer work in hospitals wherever her husband was transferred.

After being stationed around New England for a number of years, she and Merrill moved to Chicago, where Helen worked as a volunteer nurse, caring for patients at the Highland Park Hospital just north of the city, and serving as Scoutmaster for two Girl Scout Troops.

While working at Highland Park, she met Donald Able, head of a medical laboratory and a pioneer in the diagnosis and treatment of allergies, who was a patient there.

They became well acquainted while Able was under Helen's care and he urged her to work with him at his Able Medical Laboratory.

She wound up heading the laboratory's main allergy testing section and remained to help his son run the lab after Abel's death.

Becoming weary of the lab work when it grew more impersonal following the founder's death, Helen took a year off to relax at home, then departed the Chicago area after the death of her husband and headed for Maine, which she had visited frequently as a young lady.

Helen made the cross-country trip in mid-winter, towing a trailer along icy roads enroute to Cherryfield, Maine, where she purchased a home.

She made a pretty good buy. It was an eight-room house with a full basement and attic situated on two acres on a bluff overlooking a lovely river. She acquired it for $8,000.

Helen recalls that the real estate agent who sold her the house expressed concern after her arrival, noting that the houses on each side of hers were occupied by a bachelor and a divorced man.

Helen got a call the day after she moved in from a man who said he lived next door and wondered if there was anything he could do to help her.

"He had the most wonderful voice," she says. "I think I fell in love with that voice, but the only thing I could think to ask was whether he was the bachelor or the divorced neighbor."

He turned out to be Fred, who was the divorced neighbor at the time.

"We talked all night," she recalls. "We just felt we had to tell one another everything about ourselves."

That was in late December. They married in March.

After living in Cherryfield for several years, they moved to Calais, where Fred had taken the public works job.

Helen got another unanticipated job when she visited the library to check out a book, was told there was no regular librarian, and was offered the job.

"I've never applied for any job," she laughs. "I've just gotten them."

The two departed Calais, taking off on their extended camping trip when Fred quit his job.

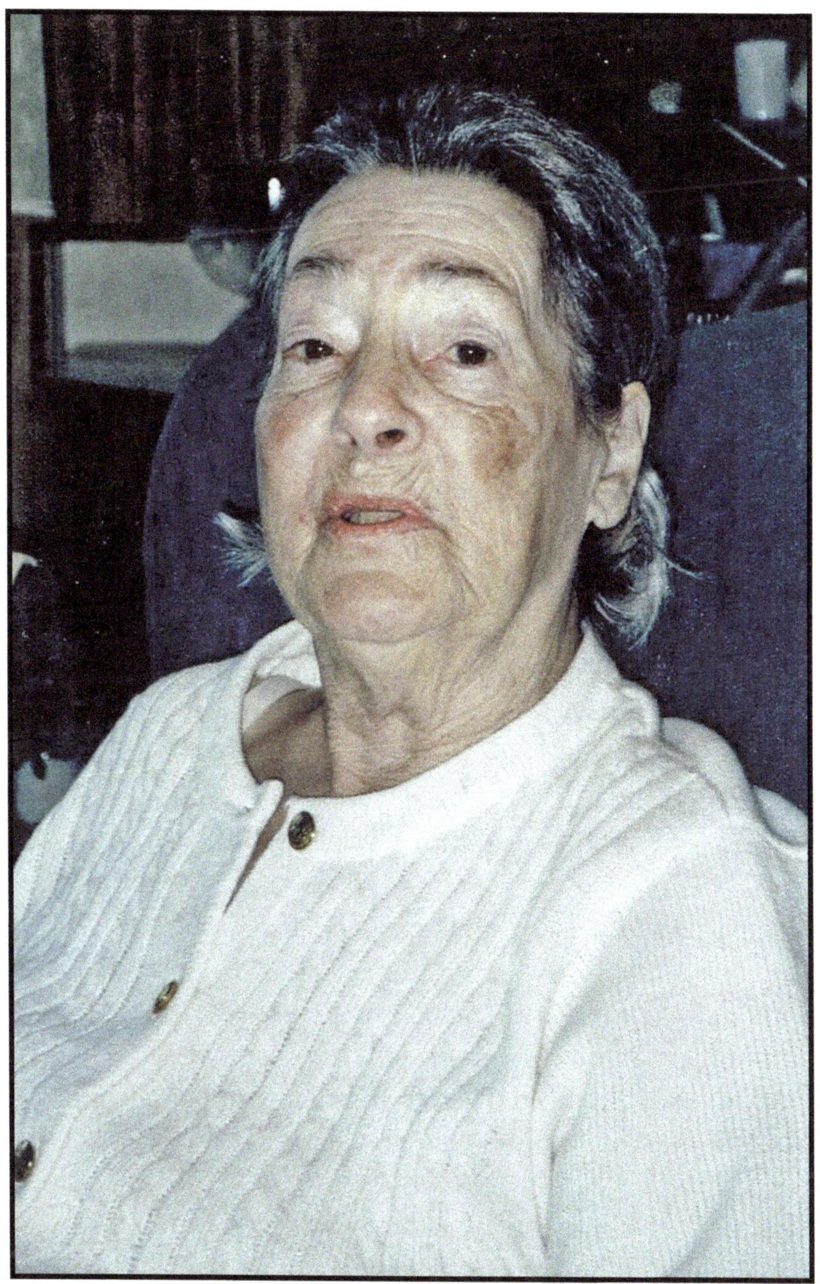

Helen Curtis discusses artic adventures.

All of Helen's tales of her Canadian adventures seem to be warm and fuzzy. She says she never felt "really cold" because the air was so dry.

"If it weren't for the permafrost the entire area would be a desert," she says.

"It was nothing like as bad as the winters I experienced in Boston."

"I remember wading through waist deep snow with my newborn baby in my arms when I headed home from the hospital. My street hadn't been cleared and the cab had no chance to make it to the house. I had to break the snow up with my body while holding the baby up around my shoulders. Winters in the Northwest Territories were much more comfortable."

After they had been in Yellowknife for ten years, the town began to grow rapidly when gold was discovered nearby and a diamond mine was about to open, making it less attractive to Fred, who came home one day to inform Helen that he had quit his job.

Her response was "Well, here we go again!"

This time they headed east until they ran out of continent and wound up in New Brunswick where they settled down in Fredericton Junction, relaxing in a little house overlooking a quiet little river.

"I could look out on the river from my kitchen window," says Helen. "It was a lovely spot."

She lingered there after Fred passed away in 1990, leaving only after her daughter, who lives just outside Atlanta, called to ask her to help her sort through some problems.

"I couldn't just say no," she says. "You couldn't live with yourself if you didn't help when they feel they need you."

Helen found herself living in a house on Norris Lake in Lithonia, but says she wasn't happy there because of the noise and the neighbors.

"There was traffic going by all the time and the people next door were some circus or carnival types," says Helen.

"They had a pickup truck with signs on it advertising a water dunking machine and they played loud music all night long. It was the wildest music you've ever heard."

She was delighted when her daughter and son-in-law purchased a house on Tybee just over a year ago and suggested that she move down.

"I just love the calm nature of the island, especially when it's foggy," she says.

"I walked down to the surf one foggy morning in a black sweater. It was covered with beads of moisture when I came back from the beach. It was like a big spider web. It reminded me of Maine and Boston. I've always loved the fog."

Helen, who is no longer as nimble as she once was, says she enjoys relaxing, reading and reflecting on her adventurous life, and believes she's finally found the perfect spot to pursue those passive passions.

POSTSCRIPT: Helen Curtis passed away in 1999 at the age of 87. Her daughter, Malinda Urvant, who still resides in the area, recalled her mother recently as an "amazing and adventurous" woman for her entire life. Malinda, who visited her mother briefly when she lived near the Artic Circle, said she, herself, couldn't tolerate the cold in that area. "Having to put on all those clothes to go outside and then take them all off when you came back was just too much," she said. "I couldn't handle that."

Ben Pearson -
Hero Gets a Surprise Present

Special Call Brings Back Memories

*O*ne of our area's decorated military heroes just got a very special early birthday present.

Col. Ben F. "Red" Pearson, who was captured after parachuting behind enemy lines in Normandy a day after the D-Day Invasion, received a phone call from a member of the family who helped him escape.

Col. Pearson, who still sports a full head of flaming red hair which is just beginning to turn gray around his temples, got the call on Feb. 3, just three weeks shy of his 83rd birthday, at the Wilmington Island residence where he and his wife, Regina, have lived since 1950.

Regina took the call for her husband. It was from the wife of a man who was just a small boy the day his family helped save the colonel's life at their French farmhouse.

Ben, who remains squarely built and rugged looking despite his years, was delighted by the "special
present" when Regina delivered the message, and he
smiled broadly while discussing the call and his harrowing escape more than 50 years ago.

Ben parachuted into a Normandy farm area with
82nd Airborne troops during the fog-shrouded night
jump and was captured along with a large group
of his comrades when hundreds of Germans troops
swooped down on them just after they landed.

Their captors lined them up in a field shortly after
daybreak where Ben says the Americans figured they
were going to be shot.

Instead, the Germans wrote down their names, took
a group photograph of their captives, and crowded

*Ben Pearson stands beside photos of his gridiron glory days
at Clemson.*

them into a farm building while awaiting orders on
what to do with them.

Ben says firewood and straw were stacked inside the
building where the men were jammed, and he wound
up in a corner in the back of the group where he buried himself under a pile of wood and straw to await
the Germans' next move.

"It seemed like a long time before they returned
because I knew I'd be shot if they found me, but it
probably wasn't more than a couple of hours," he
says.

When the Germans returned, they called each of the
prisoners' names to make sure they were all account-
ed for, and Ben arranged to have a sergeant who was
standing nearby answer for him when his was called.

Ben remained in hiding for most of the day while his
comrades were marched off to be transported to a
prison where they spent the remainder of the war.

Then, when someone approached, he removed a couple of pieces of wood and the entire pile suddenly
gave way.

Ben figured he was a goner until he realized he was
facing a Frenchman, come to gather firewood, rather
than a German soldier.

The Frenchman sneaked Ben into his house where
he shared the family's small portion of food with the
grateful American.

One of the man's several children, a daughter, had studied a bit of English and Ben was able to communicate with her in a rudimentary fashion by writing short notes.

He learned the girl's father was a pharmacist who hated the Germans, had moved his family to the farm to escape the fighting, and, while delighted to help the fugitive American, was afraid his family would be shot if Ben was found there.

Not wanting to endanger his benefactor, and hoping he was heading in the right direction to find Allied Forces, Ben set out along the dirt road in front of the farm that night.

Overcome by hunger as he traveled, he spotted some berries beside the road he couldn't identify and ate a handful, figuring at least he wouldn't die of starvation.

He hunkered down in weeds and nearby woods whenever he heard German voices.

Still ravenous, he spotted a cow near the road and, when all was quiet, found a rusty can and approached the animal, struggling to extract a cup of milk in what, in retrospect, was a rare moment of humor during his escape.

The cow turned and hooked his leather jacket, tossing him around as he cradled the hard-earned milk in his hands.

When he finally freed himself, Ben consumed the
liquid, but gave up any effort to get more. His experience was recounted later in a Columbus, Ga., newspaper which said his alma mater, Clemson University,
must be embarrassed that a graduate of that "farm
college" had never learned to milk a cow.

Ben's long journey ended when he heard weapons
being cocked as he passed a roadside barn. Before
he could run, troops descended on him shouting
"Damned!"

The word, shouted in English was music to his ears.
They were American infantrymen.

Ben joined the group, earning a Bronze Star in the
Normandy fighting before he was wounded by a bullet that lodged near his temple, and he was evacuated
to a hospital in England.

Surgeons there found the projectile was pressing
against his mastoid and that an operation to remove
it would be too dangerous. They said the war was
over for Ben, who was then a lieutenant colonel.

Ben had other ideas, however.

He donned his uniform and walked out of the hospital, joining a unit of paratroopers staging in England
and was soon back on the battlefield.

He earned a Silver Star along with clusters for his
Purple Heart for "gallantry in action against the enemy" defending against a tank attack at the Battle of
the Bulge.

His citation says Col. Pearson established a defensive position "during a retreat from overwhelming enemy forces" and when the observer's position took a direct hit, killing the officer in charge, he "carried on observation for allied artillery as enemy tanks approached, personally directing the fire of tank destroyers in his area, exposing himself to enemy fire without regard to personal safety."

Ben was badly wounded and sent back to a hospital in England when his jeep was demolished by a land mine later in the fighting.

He suffered multiple leg injuries so severe that surgeons said they would have to amputate both legs.

Again, Ben had other ideas.

"If I'm going to have to lose them it will be in the United States, not in England," he declared.

Ben was shipped back to the U.S. aboard the Queen Mary, which had been converted to a hospital ship transporting thousands of wounded GIs.

While aboard, a nurse, assisted by a soldier on crutches whose legs had been amputated, passed by his bunk when she was giving shots to the wounded men.

"Right then I realized how really lucky I was," says Ben.

He wound up in a hospital in Augusta, Ga. where he remained for months undergoing repeated operations.

Regina and Ben Pearson discuss early days.

Miraculously, surgeons said, he recovered from his wounds, although he still has a deep gouge in his right leg and that bullet remains lodged in his head.

It was while recovering in Augusta that he met Regina, who had come up from her home in Camilla, Ga., to spend time with her brother who was graduating from the University of Georgia Medical School.

Regina says Camilla had become a virtual ghost town because all its young people had gone to war and she wanted to spend time with her brother before he, too, shipped out.

She had just turned 20 when she and another young woman agreed to take on the task of operating a hospitality house for wounded soldiers, providing coffee, cookies, and a smiling face in those desperate times.

A friend of Ben urged Regina to go on a blind date with his buddy, but when she asked if he "was another one of those Clemson boys" the friend had to confess that he was, and she declined.

Ben had indeed been a "Clemson boy" prior to the war, going there on a football scholarship and becoming a gridiron star, playing running and blocking back for four years.

"We beat Carolina (the University of South Carolina) every time we played them," says Ben, noting that he still thinks his Clemson coach, Jess Neely, was one of the best.

In his senior year, Ben played on a bowl-winning team and says he still remembers "what a thrill it was" playing before thousands of fans in the Florida stadium.

"It made me want to be my very best," he says.

He also remembers an opponent who roughed him up on a tackle, making him so mad Ben says he "kicked him in his butt" during an ensuing scuffle.

Despite his gridiron heroics, Regina was not impressed. She says she had just been out with one graduate of Clemson and was not interested in meeting anymore.

Recalling the event now she laughs and says she was kidding, and that the Clemson boys were not that bad.

Later, Ben's friend "dared" her to go out with Ben, but again she demurred.

"Then he double dared me and promised I'd be all right since the date would consist of dinner with him and his wife at their home," she says. "I'd never been double dared before, so I agreed."

It was the friend who climbed the three flights of stairs to fetch Regina for the date that night, noting, offhand, that Ben couldn't handle the stairs.

She learned when she reached the car that Ben wore a full cast on one leg, a half cast on the other, and was hobbling about on crutches.

"Their yard was covered with mud when we got to the house," she recalls, noting that she was wearing a dressy green outfit for the occasion and her host gallantly offered to carry her across the yard to avoid the mud.

"I'm damned if you do, she's my date!" Regina quotes her future husband as saying. "And Ben carried me across that yard under his arm, dragging himself through the mud on those crutches!"

Ben asked her to marry him on their second date, but she held out until the fourth. They were married May 1, 1946, just two weeks after they met.

The newlyweds really got to know each other after Ben's casts came off and they took an extended cross-country drive filled with misadventures.

Regina says somewhere in Montana, he swerved their car from the road and headed off across a field, claiming he wanted her to see a buffalo when she demanded to know what he was doing.

"The car mired down in the field up to the hubcaps, and while Ben was trying to dig it out with his hands, a buffalo walked up and licked me across the face," she laughs. "I got to see a buffalo all right."

Then the car's horn got stuck and wouldn't stop blowing while they were passing through a small town.

When Ben pulled over and jumped out to raise the hood to disconnect it, his pants fell down (he had unbuttoned them, seeking relief while driving, having gained weight during those months in the hospital without exercise, and outgrown his trousers).

Regina says she was convulsed with laughter when a woman pushing a baby carriage approached with a horrified look on her face as Ben groped for his fallen trousers.

"Ben just kept yelling for me to get him a screwdriver before the battery died," she says. "You couldn't get batteries or tires in those days and few people except those in the military could even get gas."

"Ben was really upset, but I can't tell you how funny he looked!"

On another occasion they had a flat tire and the trunk lid smashed down on Ben's head when he reached for the spare.

"Blood was pouring down his face, but he changed the tire and refused to let me drive when he started up again," says Regina. "I told him he needed to hold a rag on his head to stop the bleeding, but he said he couldn't do that and drive too!"

"Then it started raining and we drove for miles before we found a little hotel. Ben went in and got a room but told me the people acted really strange and he was concerned. I said, 'Just look at yourself, Ben!' The rain had reopened the wound on his head and blood was pouring down his face and shirt."

Regina learned a bit about Ben's playful side when they decided to go horseback riding during another stopover.

Regina was reluctantly placed on a docile animal while Ben mounted a highly spirited horse, and when she complained he traded with her, then whacked the high-strung horse on the rump just after she mounted.

"It took off galloping and kept on going, sailing over a crevice that was so deep you couldn't see the bottom of it, while I kept screaming, Whoa, Suh!" recalls Regina.

"When I finally got it stopped, I was shaking and Ben came up laughing like the devil and asking me what the heck 'Whoa, Suh' meant. I told him it meant I wanted the horse to stop!"

During their six-week trip they visited the military base in Nebraska where Ben underwent parachute training after receiving his commission at Fort Benning. (Ben was assigned to the 507th Parachute Infantry and, as a major, became operations officer of his regiment before being reassigned to the 82nd airborne).

Ben had a narrow escape while making a jump over a lake during his training at the base when his chute failed to fully open. He was knocked unconscious when he hit the water and had to be pulled out.

Regina Pearson stands beside some of Ben's medals from World War II.

They later visited Fort Benning, where Regina says she got her own discomfiting taste of parachute jumping.

An officer's wife insisted that Regina make a training jump, saying this was a custom for the wives of paratroopers.

"She said it would embarrass Ben if I didn't jump," according to Regina, who says she stayed up all night worrying before finally agreeing to do it.

"They took me up to the jump training tower and had me sign a release before I went so they wouldn't be responsible. That was one of the scariest things I've ever been through."

"I'd tried a parachute jump thing at the World's Fair before, but it was nothing like this one. I don't know if Ben was proud of me or not, but it was frightening!"

The woman who prompted Regina to jump later admitted that she had never done it and had no intention of doing such a crazy thing.

Both Regina and Ben agree that as newlyweds they had become much better acquainted by the time they returned East following their honeymoon trip.

Soon after their return, Ben was discharged due to his disabilities and they moved to Savannah, his childhood home.

Although she loved Savannah, Regina says she hated the duplex they had to settle in, "because housing was almost impossible to find. Ben told me not to complain, that it was all we could get."

It soon became clear, despite all the revelations on the trip, that Ben didn't know his wife that well at the time.

She secretly arranged to have a real estate salesman show them a Wilmington Island house she saw listed in the newspaper and lured Ben out to the property on one of their weekend trips to Tybee.

"It seemed like it took forever to get there," she says. "It (Wilmington Island Road) was just a little dirt road at the time" and the house was located far out at the eastern end, where it joins Walthour Road."

"I got really scared as we approached the house, and he asked me if it was for sale. I had to admit that it was and that a real estate salesman was waiting for us."

"Then, after we looked around, I asked the salesman to wait while Ben and I went upstairs to talk."

"When we got up there, I told Ben I really wanted the house and he said, 'Well I do too, and we'll get it if you'll just shut up!' Boy, was I relieved! I didn't open my mouth again."

That was in 1950 and the Pearsons have lived there ever since.

The original part of their home on Half Moon River was constructed in the 1930s with logs floated over and hauled up the riverbank by dray horses. The Pearsons still keep a pair of the oversized horseshoes from those huge horses on their mantelpiece.

The house was originally built for an artist who designed the ornately patterned wood floors and used a different design for each room.

The numerous medals and citations Ben received for his heroism during the war are mounted on a wall beside the living room staircase.

Included in the display is a picture of Ben's grandfather, who was just 12 years old when he joined Confederate troops as an aide during the Civil War.

Regina and Ben have added to the house over the years and have raised their three children there.

After 23 years' employment with Wesson Oil Co. Ben retired in 1973 just before showing up at their home by surprise one day.

"What are you doing here at lunch time?" Regina says she asked when Ben appeared at the door. "You don't think I'm making your lunch, do you?"

"I just retired, is that OK?" Ben replied timidly.

"I've never seen him happier than when he was finally able to sit out on the patio and read the newspaper and just relax and look around," says Regina.

Ben has become an avid fisherman over the years.

"He went fishing every weekend while I took the children to church," says Regina, who attended the old non-denominational Mission Church, which burned down in the 1970s. It was the first church established on Wilmington Island, according to Regina.

She says she finally tricked her husband into joining her at church by saying she was tired of taking their children by herself and no longer planned to attend services.

"We stayed home for about three weeks, and he finally got embarrassed and insisted that we all go together," she laughs.

"He became quite active after that and was one of the founders of the Wilmington Island Presbyterian Church, which we still attend."

Regina says the son of the French pharmacist who helped Ben married an American woman and it was she who made the surprise phone call just before Ben's birthday while visiting in North Carolina.

"She said her father-in-law, the man who saved Ben in Normandy, opened a pharmacy which is still in operation in a little town near his farm after the war."

"We're planning to correspond now, and I asked her to get a picture of the house where they took Ben in and the barn where he hid, if it is still standing."

"You know, we've had a wonderful life, and if it weren't for that family, Ben might never have been here to enjoy it."

POSTSCRIPT: Ben F. Pearson was 84 when he passed away on June 19, 1999. His wife, Regina Hackett Pearson, died Dec. 22, 2006. She was 85.

Rick and Debbie Sheridan -
Couple Anchors Island Music Scene

Busily Awaiting Big Break

*J*ust call 'em Rick and Debbie, these two expatriates from Birmingham, Ala. who have been anchoring the music scene on Tybee for the past six years.

"Anchoring" is not just a nautical term for a beach story. Rick and Debbie Sheridan are credited by virtually every professional musician on the island with having encouraged and worked with them to hone their skills.

"They've given their time, effort and talent to make us all better at what we do," says Charlie Sherrill, who played with Rick and Debbie for three years before finding his own niche as house musician at Doc's Bar on Tybee's south end and is now one of the island's most popular performers.

Debbie, who has written more than a hundred original songs, harbors dreams of making it big as a writer/performer. She's been spending a lot to time recording her songs in a small home studio, sending her material out... and hoping.

Their weekend band, *The Nxchange,* gets frequent re-
quests to play her compositions at the DeSoto Beach
Hotel's indoor bar and outdoor dance floor, but thus
far nothing has really jelled for her in the off-island
music industry.

"Still," says Rick, "you never know when it will click,
and Debbie's ready!"

Rick, who's obviously self-effacing, introduced Debbie to work as a professional musician after offering
her instruction on a keyboard.

She took to the instrument immediately, excelling to
the point where Rick now says "Debbie's the star of
the show. She's the real talent."

They perform as a duo on Wednesday and Thursday
at the DeSoto's indoor lounge and are joined by John
O'Neill on drums and James Moody on saxophone to
become *The Nxchange* band each weekend atop the
hotel's outside bandstand.

Both Sheridans were raised in Birmingham.

Debbie's initial exposure to music was singing in the
choir of a Baptist church and plunking tentatively on
an old guitar while experimenting with writing songs.

Rick came by his musical talent naturally. His father
was a professional musician leading a band called
Hard Times and bringing Rick into the group as a
drummer for weekend gigs in Birmingham.

Rick and Debbie check beach beside the DeSoto.

When his father, who played bass, passed away at age 41, Rick took his place as both band leader and bass player performing mostly on weekends.

But Rick's first "regular job" was far from any band stand. He worked as a coal miner in Alabama strip mines for a while before spending eleven years on the road driving an 18-wheeler.

That occupation ended abruptly when Rick suffered a broken neck in a waterskiing accident and was laid up for almost a year.

After his recovery he decided to try to make it in music full time and has been doing just that, quite successfully, ever since.

Debbie and Rick got together when he was interviewing singers to front his band. She auditioned and not only won the job but Rick's heart. They've been married for 15 years.

"But the music scene was tough in Birmingham," says Rick. "Clubs where we wanted to play started demanding that the vocalist not only sing but play an instrument as well."

That's when he introduced Debbie to an organ keyboard and provided her initial instruction.

She was such a quick study she was soon performing beyond Rick's range, polishing her musicianship by attending a music school in Birmingham, and becoming almost fanatical about practice.

Her accomplished keyboard technique enabled her to emulate the sounds of numerous instruments to cover for less reliable musicians who disdained those lengthy practice sessions.

After hiring an agent, they hit the Holiday Inn circuit, playing in lounges all over the country, first in two-week engagements and ultimately for two or

Debbie in the spotlight behind keyboard.

three months at each location.

Rick says they called the band *The Exchange* back then because there was so much turnover among the musicians they hired.

The *Nxchange* name was adopted when they came to Tybee, determined to bring permanent sidemen aboard.

It was at a Holiday Inn appearance in Aberdeen, S.D. that they faced the first of a couple of near disasters.

"They were putting on an all-male review and we were playing before and after the act," Rick recalls.

"One night all these guys were dancing and mingling with the crowd of about 350 women when somebody tossed a smoke bomb into the room."

"The place turned into a stampede with everybody scrambling outside, into knee-deep snow, semi-nude men, middle-aged women and all!"

Hunkering down in a corner until the smoke cleared, Rick and Debbie managed to escape injury but, unlike the usual smoke-filled rooms where they had performed, this one brought their gig to a quick end.

Not long after that, they were booked aboard the cruise ship S.S. Norway touring The Caribbean, but that engagement lasted only a month when it was upset by another unexpected event...one in which "upset" was the operable word.

Rick and Debbie are joined by Charlie Sherrill, center, on DeSoto Beach Hotel bandstand.

"We found that Debbie got seasick, no matter how calm the water was, and she just couldn't handle it, so we had to give it up," says Rick wistfully. (He's a big man who's obviously missed very few meals, and despite his guilt over Debbie's queasy condition, he relished those expansive shipboard buffets.)

The two were back doing the Holiday Inn tour when they were booked for a weekend at Tybee's DeSoto Beach hotel, where they were an immediate hit, drew large crowds, and they were offered the regular weekend booking.

That was six years ago and, tired of those constant road trips, they've been here ever since, expanding their appearances to five nights a week and becoming established as the DeSoto's house musicians.

"Wednesday and Thursday used to draw huge crowds but the customers dwindled considerably after two bad automobile accidents" on Highway 80 on consecutive nights, according to Rick.

After those wrecks roadblocks were set up on the highway almost every night to check for drunk drivers and people became reluctant to drive out from Savannah.

Only when the hotel books big name bands like *The Tams, The Platters, The Coasters, or Rare Earth* do Rick and Debbie take a back seat as performers, and even then they serve as the introductory act, and

Debbie Sheridan is waiting for her big break.

Rick handles the sound and lighting for the featured entertainers.

Three years ago, they started what has become the regular Sunday night talent contest in which amateur and professional

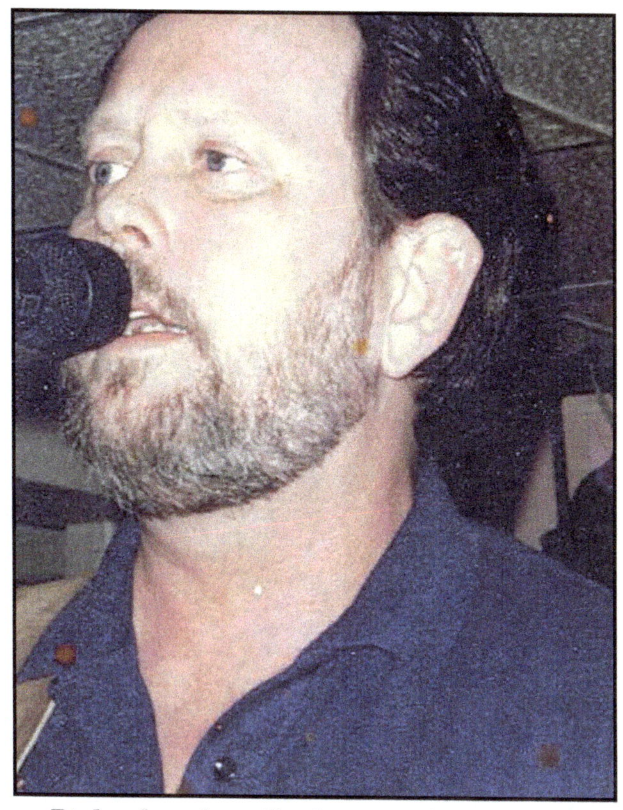

Rick takes the mike during talent contest.

singers, musicians, comedians, dancers, and even a popular island purveyor of bird calls participate each week throughout the summer.

Hundreds gather for the contest on the outside dance floor each Sunday evening, with weekly winners participating in a gala final contest on Labor Day Sunday.

Shortly after arriving at the beach, Rick and Debbie also developed a mutual interest in something other than music.

They became avid fishermen.

"That's the thing we liked most about Tybee... the fishing," says Rick.

They acquired a couple of boats and have become adept at landing the big ones.

Rick says he learned to rig and bait his lines from an expert local fisherman, but he refuses to disclose the technique because "it's a closely guarded secret."

Rick and Debbie perform at DeSoto Beach Hotel.

The great times they had fishing - "we'd be out every day we had off," says Rick - have been severely curtailed of late, however, since Rick has been made a manager at the DeSoto Beach Hotel, which leaves little time for angling.

Like so many others who've come for a visit and lingered, the Sheridans now have Tybee's sand twixt their toes and have no plans to leave.

"We'll certainly be here until our daughter, Lynn, who's now 12, finishes school," and likely much longer, says Debbie.

Even if that longed for recording contract materializes, "this will be our home base," said Rick recently as he and Debbie dashed off on an unusually slow Tuesday for one of their now rare afternoons of fishing.

POSTSCRIPT: Rick and Debbie departed the Tybee music scene after the famous old DeSoto Beach Hotel was demolished. They continued performing for a couple of years in the DeSoto Hotel in downtown Savannah, and at other area venues. Debbie says when hauling their equipment around and setting it up and taking it down for one-night stands became a burden and the music scene seemed to be shrinking they moved down to Shellman's Bluff in McIntosh County. They continued performing intermittently, but Rick ultimately returned to his old truck-driving trade to bring in a steady income. He passed away of a heart attack in 2014 after pulling his big rig into a truck stop in Orange, Texas where he was found collapsed at the wheel after his rig rolled slowly into another truck. Following his death, Debbie moved to Bloomingdale where she says, despite never having gotten that big break in music, she is now contented and living comfortably with her pets, a dog and a cat, in a house surrounded by the flower, vegetable, and herb gardens she loves. She continues to get in a bit of fishing and recently participated in a memorial tournament on Tybee. The Sheridan's daughter, Lynn, grew up, married, and still resides on the island.

Linnie Youngblood -
Industrious Lady at Home on Water

Fishing
Fits Her
Lifestyle

*S*he was born to fish - been an avid angler all her life - and she's finally found the spot where she can pursue that passion any time she wants.

Linnie Elizabeth Youngblood is the "Lin" half of Tybee's MarLin Marina, which she owns with partner Marian Ladner, a Savannah attorney.

Georgia born and bred, Linnie's lineage goes back even further than those elitists who claim to have ancestors who sailed to Savannah to settle the area with Gen. Oglethorpe.

Her grandmother was a quarter Cherokee Indian, and it was she for whom Linnie is named.

"She was a tough woman who had 11 children," says Linnie. "I guess that's where I get my stamina from. I thought a lot of her. My parents knew she was a great woman."

Of his four daughters, it was Linnie who inherited her father's passion for fishing.

"I was the one who ran the boat for my dad and did all the cleanup work," she smiles.

Linnie smiles frequently, sprinkling rays of sunshine around on the cloudiest of days.

Before she was old enough for school, she would join her father on the Chattahoochee River and Lake Eufaula, near their home in Columbus, Ga., where they would wet their lines, regardless of rain, sleet or whatever.

"I've gone fishing when it was 20 degrees," says Linnie. "I've always been in love with the sport and if the fish were biting, I didn't care what the weather was like."

Mostly they were fishing

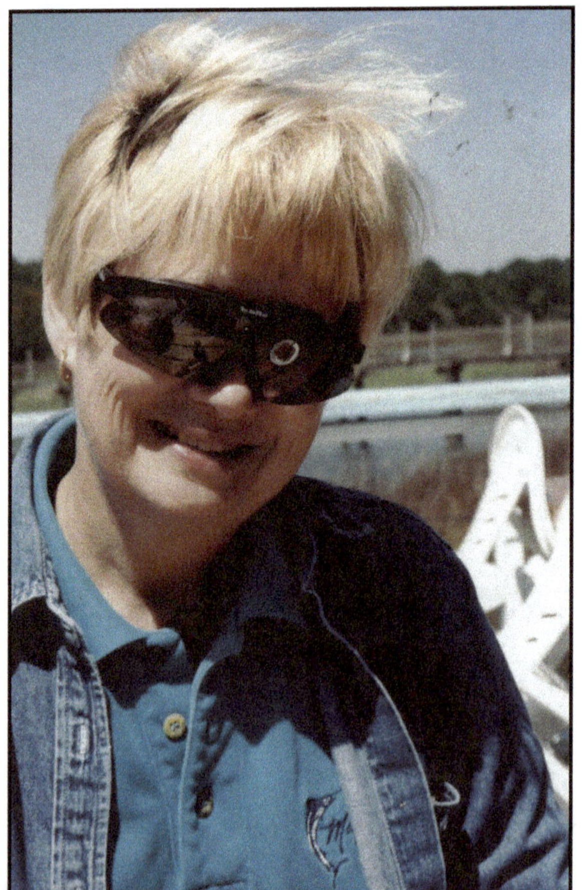

Linnie Youngblood smiling as usual.

for bass with artificial lures back in her freshwater fishing days.

She also became adept at making jewelry while in Columbus and pursued that craft for several years, but it was fishing that hooked her heart.

Her reputation was such that while still a teenager she was approached by a professional bass fishing team that tried to entice her to join them touring the country, trolling for big money.

It was the touring part that turned her off. Linnie liked lingering beside familiar waters and declined their offer.

Now she can head for the water whenever she wants and never misses a week without getting out at least once all by herself.

Most days she spends serving as a fishing guide or conducting dolphin-watching tours on the river and sea surrounding Tybee, or performing the myriad duties required around a marina.

Linnie discovered Tybee as a child when her family brought her along on their frequent trips to the island whose beauty, along with the accepting nature of its residents, made an indelible impression, inexorably luring her back through the years.

Linnie is a lady with numerous abilities in addition to those she displays at her marina.

After completing a couple of years at Columbus College, she decided it was time to try her wings and
took off for Clarksville, Tenn., where she worked for
an electronics firm, assembling computer compo-
nents, and building the metal cabinets in which they
were housed.

It was there that she learned to work with sheet
metal, putting her in good stead for her subsequent
employment at Gulfstream, a position that pulled her
closer to her dream of living on Tybee.

Linnie, who says she's never been intimidated by any
problem nor found anything she couldn't learn to do,
proved her point repeatedly in that job.

She learned aircraft assembly and installation on
light airplanes at Gulfstream, working mostly with
sheet metal, which was far afield from making jewelry
and fishing lures.

Later she was assigned to purchasing and expediting
parts acquisition.

Gulfstream's location in Savannah and its proximity
to Tybee enabled her to come out frequently.

Linnie eventually purchased a house on the island,
and she started spending spare time around a small
marina on the Back River. It was this marina that
she ultimately purchased.

Along the way she acquired her master's license, per-
mitting her to conduct commercial fishing and sight-

seeing excursions from the marina on weekends.

After 13 years with Gulfstream "I'd had enough of corporate garbage," she says, still smiling.

That's when Linnie decided it was time to get back to water, which was her real love.

She went into marine sales in Maryland, working around the western shore of the Chesapeake Bay from Annapolis south to Lexington Park, delivering boats to her customers by both land and sea.

Linnie lingered at that job for four years, but she still harbored memories of the little Tybee marina and finally returned to purchase the facility when it came on the market in 1994.

You can find Linnie around the place almost any time nowadays.

She'll be the athletic blonde lady crawling around, under and on top of boats making repairs or manning the electric hoist to launch or haul them from the water, smiling all the while.

Make no mistake, however, behind that pleasant smile is a serious Linnie who really knows her stuff.

She provides advice to skippers on repairs or fittings that need replacing on their watercraft, or safety, or virtually any other aspect of boats and boating.

Most of the wise ones take her advice.

Some don't.

Take, for instance, the guy who set out from the marina on a camping trip to a nearby island not long ago.

Linnie warned him that his little boat was overloaded with gear, and he might run into trouble when he headed into the wind-blown incoming tide off Little Tybee Island across the Back River.

He pooh-poohed her advice, saying he had made the run a number of times and Linnie was being unnecessarily cautious.

Less than an hour later his boat swamped, and he lost most of his equipment in the area Linnie had warned him about.

The macho mariner was hang-dog repentant after bailing out his boat and returning to her dock.

In her spare time, Linnie putters around her dockside shop doing carpentry work and repairing motors and other marina machinery.

She also designs and builds "animal chairs" for children.

Linnie decorates the wooden chairs with different animals carved in relief and painted.

She also teaches children the art of fishing and sponsors a tournament for youngsters 2 to 13 years old each year.

Linnie conducts day trips as a fishing and dol-
phin-viewing guide whenever she can, but given her
endless chores, from launching and hauling boats to
working below floating docks, running and repairing
water lines and operating the ship's store as well as
supervising activities in the marina restaurant, she
has precious little time for these.

Linnie Youngblood displays chairs she crafted.

The industrious marina operator has consistently improved the MarLin since becoming its co-owner.

It now sports a beefed-up hoist that can handle boats up to 27 feet and features an excellent restaurant with a recently installed full-service kitchen.

An outside dining area adjoining the restaurant has been expanded to the dock, offering diners a breathtaking view of sunsets over the marsh with their meals.

Last year Linnie incorporated live music on weekends, hiring popular island saxophonist and singer Harvey Ray, who proved an immediate hit and has been brought back again this year.

Her dream is to make the marina better each year and she seems to be right on schedule.

Linnie can't imagine being any other place. The marina is her home and has clearly captured her heart. Her obvious joy is as infectious as her constant smile.

POSTSCRIPT: Linnie Youngblood, who turned 72 in 2023 and is now retired, moved to Englewood on Florida's west coast in 2009. Her home there suffered severe damage from Hurricane Ian in 2022 and Linnie kept busy making repairs. She still enjoys fishing, mostly close to shore these days, but was making plans not long ago to travel south to the Keys where she hoped to do some offshore angling.

Roger Dodge -
Loveable 'Collector' Covers Tybee

Recycling
Amid Some
Tall Tales

*W*hile they call him by different names - Roger Dodge, or Roger the Dodger, or Rog the Dodge, among them - or don't call him at all (it seems of little consequence to him) virtually everyone on Tybee knows Roger.

He traverses the island at all hours of the day and night and-deeply tanned and deceptively hard bodied, despite an honestly-earned beer belly, and sporting a halo of curling, sun-bleached hair blending into a curly beard-he's difficult to overlook.

Day folks assume he's just another city employee.

They see him cutting the grass along Butler Avenue and around public buildings, and, if they're up early enough, they may see him working on a city trash truck, beginning about 7:30.

Roger says he cuts the grass whenever and wherever it's needed.

The trash truck he works on looks a little like Roger himself. It's a round, hard-bodied vehicle with doors on each side that you can see through when they're open.

Roger Dodge collects cans for recycling.

Roger usually fills one of the doors when the truck is in motion, standing spreadeagled in the opening while shouting greetings to everyone he passes during the truck's circuitous route around city-owned property.

When there's a need, he also works on a water truck.

And then there is the after-hours Roger.

Around midnight, particularly on weekends, you can find him wandering around the island's night spots and along the south-end beachfront parking lot.

Roger helps out at several bars, doing the heavy lifting and emptying trash, and when the bar business slows down early in the morning, you'll see him combing through the trash bins outside, collecting aluminum cans and bagging them for recycling to make extra money.

"It's a right good little business," he says. "It gets real good when the price gets up to around 65 cents a pound" for aluminum.

Currently, it's far below that, he laments, but regardless of the price, you can forget about getting into this sideline yourself, at least on Tybee.

Roger doesn't want anyone horning in on his recycling business and has had conflicts with several would-be interlopers. He let them know quite forcefully that they were in the wrong area. He's particularly averse to collectors who slip out to the island from Savannah.

"Those guys ought to just stay in Savannah," he
growls. "They got no right out here, and I tell 'em so,
too."

Those who are not easily discouraged have found that
Roger, who is normally a pleasant, laid-back individual, can play hard ball, and he wins most of his argu-
ments.

Roger also does a bit of work around shrimp boats
when things are slow and has been known to repair
equipment and bicycles on request using various odds
and ends he picks up on his rounds.

The yard at his house on the south end is a maze of
rusting pieces of machinery and assorted lumps and
clumps of things, including what used to be a big
boat.

The question many people who see him in action day
and night ask is when does he sleep?

"I get enough for me," Roger responds simply.

According to those who know him best, however, one
does have to be a bit cautious about accepting everything he says at face value.

Roger has claimed his real business is owning a large
fleet of watercraft, including eight large shrimp boats
docked at the Lazaretto Creek Marina and 30 small
boats which he keeps on trailers and rents out to commercial fishermen.

"I've got a whole bunch of money," he offered gratuitously, during a recent conversation with me.

Since this seemed somewhat strange for a trashman, I checked with several shrimp boat owners around Lazaretto. All said they knew Roger and laughed at my gullibility when I asked where his boats were located.

One did say Roger might have an old, wrecked boat somewhere, but he knew of nothing Roger owned that was seaworthy.

Several islanders just grinned and said: "That's Roger, alright."

His sister, Debbie, who works at the Outback Cafe on the north end of Tybee, said that if her brother owned any shrimp boats "it's news to me. The only boat he's got that I know of is that old, wrecked

Roger gives thumbs up though trash truck opening.

197

thing in his yard. You've just got to understand that
Roger is Roger."

Despite his seemingly cavalier connection with verac-
ity, everyone who knows him speaks of Roger with
genuine affection.

"He's just a really nice guy," is the most frequent
response you get when you ask long-time residents

Roger gets ready for trash run.

about Roger Dodge. That, and "He's a sweetheart," from most of the women who know him.

One young woman who passed by during our sidewalk conversation asked Roger if he would help her if she needed it.

"I'd kill for you," he vowed, and from the sound of his voice you think he might be serious.

Then, when he learned that she and her boyfriend needed a place to stay, he offered them space in his house.

Roger says he has been married twice (his sister confirms this) "and I ain't gonna do it again. All them women want is your money, and I ain't gonna let them have any more."

The money thing, including his claim of affluence, may not be far from the truth, according to several islanders who say Roger "never spends a nickel. He drinks free at local bars in return for the chores he does, and he's probably got a bunch in the bank, just like he claims."

One long-time acquaintance said Roger saves all the bottle tops he finds and uses the prize stamps inside to get free soft drinks, and "if he doesn't have a bottle cap for a free soda, he'll drink water."

Roger himself, admits that he rarely pays for his drinks; he does his own cooking to save on food costs, and he puts virtually all his money in the bank.

The speculation regarding Roger's thrift became easier to believe one morning recently when he laughed uproariously while rummaging through the rubbish inside the trash truck he was working on, and you figured he'd found a winning lottery ticket or a hundred-dollar bill.

What he actually found was a coupon for a free hamburger which he quickly tucked away in his trousers.

It was a banner day for Rog the Dodge. He had himself another free meal.

POSTSCRIPT: Still a beloved island character, Roger Dodge was reportedly 78 years old when he passed away last year. That derelict boat, along with the eclectic mix of junk, trash and antiques that lingered for years in the yard of his south end house were cleared away recently and I-beams were installed under the top floor. Workmen at the site said the top floor of the house is being raised to install a new ground floor beneath it. Roger's sister, Deborah Dodge Loupasis, passed away in 2015, and no one seems to know if Roger really left a fortune somewhere. That remains a mystery, as does an old island incident long-time island insiders indicate may have involved Roger. Most agree that this and other prickly island mysteries were best laid to rest with their old friend.

Jim Carter -
Finds Lighthouse by Design

Stays Busy
With Crafts,
Helping Friends

*J*immy Carter - not the former President/farmer but the former electrician/craftsman - has found his specialty beneath Tybee's Lighthouse.

Well, he's not exactly under it, but just a stone's throw away at his shop behind Officers Row in Ft. Screven.

Lighthouses are his specialty.

Carter has been dabbling with crafts for more than a dozen years, beginning back when he worked with the electric company in Jacksonville.

That's when he started a spare-time hobby making windchimes from old bottles.

After retiring and returning to Tybee (he grew up on the island, leaving to serve as a U.S. Marine and later becoming an electrician in Florida), he became seriously involved in crafts as a profession.

Initially, Carter continued cutting glass bottles and making windchimes, then expanded into crafting boats and other items which he installed in sealed bottles, then started designing and building wooden airplanes and other models for area residents.

But when he started building lighthouses - replicas of authentic old lights in various areas, but most prominently the historic Tybee Lighthouse itself - he found that he not only enjoyed it enormously, but his business suddenly developed a backlog of orders.

Jimmy Carter with lighthouse he built.

"I have trouble keeping up with them now," he smiles, while working in his shop.

He is currently making night lights, bird feeders, glass-encased models and even wind-chimes in the form of lighthouses and always has orders for more.

All of his business comes from word of mouth or the island craft shows in which he participates.

He is currently working extra-long hours trying to get a few pieces ahead to participate in a "Celebration of

One of Carter's craft projects - a cigarette pack in a street light bulb.

the Arts on Tybee" Oct. 11 and 12, sponsored by the Tybee Arts Assn. The exhibition, to be held on the island's new Pavilion, will feature juried arts, fine crafts, music and dance.

Carter is also putting the final touches on a large lighthouse model in the middle of his backyard.

Friends call his yard a "golf course" since he has set up a little pitch-and-putt layout there where a regular group gathers on Sundays for what could be loosely called golf but more accurately dubbed conviviality (there's more quaffing and conversation than golf).

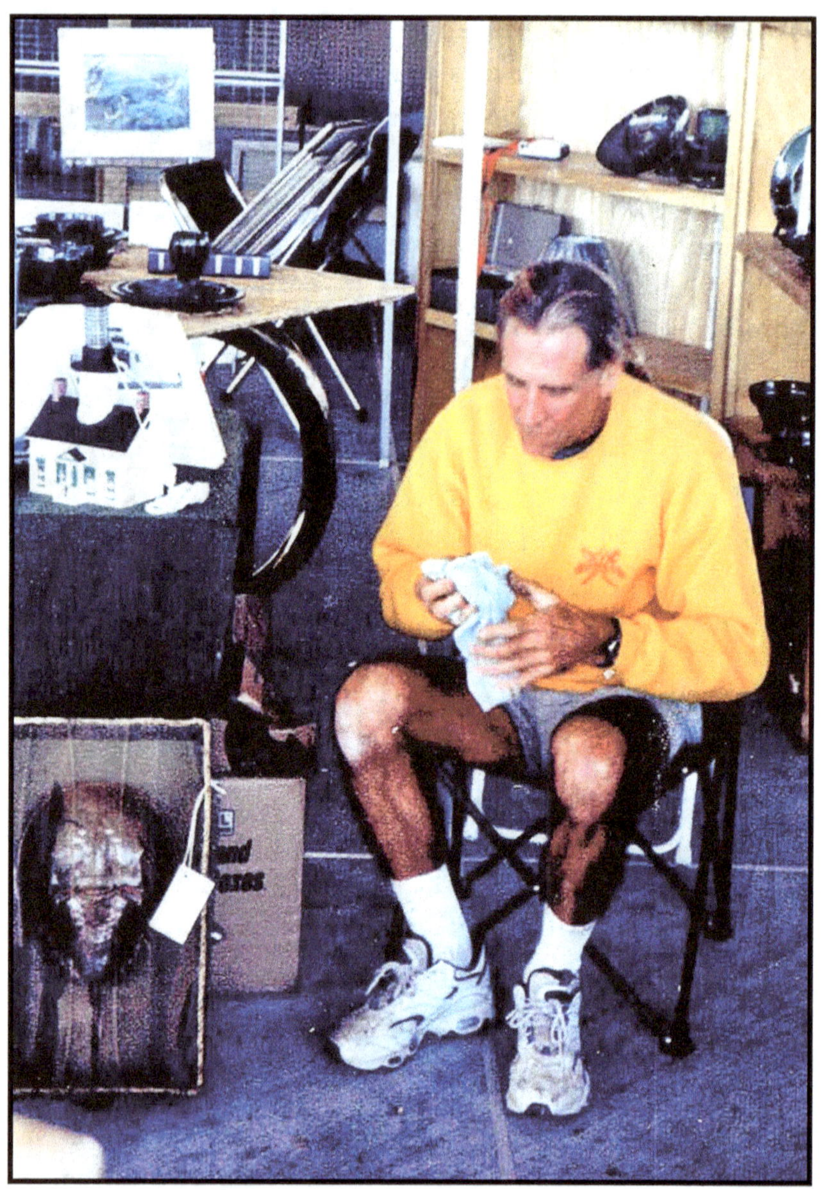

Carter polishes crafts in his shop.

This lighthouse is situated in the center of the "golf course," and he is tentatively planning to install floodlights in the top lighting chamber which will enable his friends to continue playing after dark on warm summer evenings.

Carter can count most island residents as his friends.
Not only is his home a weekend gathering place, but
he is one of the most gregarious and helpful people on
Tybee.

That's another reason for his backlog. He constantly
takes breaks from his workshop to help the seemingly
endless stream of people who solicit his assistance to
solve electrical, automotive, motorcycle, boat, tile,
plumbing and other problems on which he is a wiz-
ard.

The light of his generosity and that of his model
lighthouses are always glowing somewhere on the
island.

...Hosts Hidden Tybee "Golf Course"

Golf on Tybee? Not the miniature stuff, but the real
thing?

Listen carefully. It's a closely guarded secret. There's
a golf PGA course on the island!

It's a nine-hole layout and it's private, but it's there,
right beside the picturesque marsh of Horse Pen
Creek. You could spot it from Highway 80 if you
knew where to look.

The course seems as popular as the Masters for a boisterous bunch of good ole boys and girls on Sunday afternoons when, like most exclusive courses, it sports a long wait to get a tee time.

The layout, the Carter Golf and Country Club, is officially certified by the PGA (The Pathetic Golfer's Association).

Members don't worry about the long wait to play. Sitting and sipping; the latter, voraciously, is a principal part of the fun.

They munch from delicious platters of food brought there by the members themselves, in addition to goodies provided by course owners Jim and Barbara Carter.

While waiting and imbibing, the loquacious spectators sprawl in the shade of trees and umbrellas hurl-

Edwin Longwater, left, watches J.R.'s stroke during competition.

ing good-natured verbal barbs at one another and at those on the course.

This is not your typical Augusta National crowd. These folks have a lot more fun.

The spectators' view is spectacular. It's like that from the Goodyear blimp since you can see the entire golf course from any location.

Like a short par three hole, this course is only about 150 yards… in all… back and forth across the yard behind the Carter house.

The course itself is never crowded because with the fairways crisscrossing continually, only one foursome at a time can play.

But don't laugh! Each hole is as tough a par three as any wannabe Greg Norman or Freddy Couples would care to play.

Players use regular wedges, seven irons and putters, all provided by their hosts.

The layout features fairways that are, literally, rough. They're covered with three-inch high sawgrass on which even well-hit balls bounce and bury. You can give up on getting any kind of consistent roll.

And the greens? Forget about lobbing a lovely flop shot and having it stick by the cup. If you're into masochism, you'll love these babies!

"Babies" is no misnomer. No green is more than two feet wide.

These greens, appropriately, consist of green indoor/outdoor carpeting, and they undulate because of the uneven ground beneath them. Frequently, players have to lift and shake the carpet to clear debris, but this incurs no penalty.

The Carters' little layout also has sand traps, a water hole and horrendous, thigh-high rough surrounding it.

Like any good layout, the course is continually being improved.

The greens were originally mounds of dirt with flowerpots sunk in them for cups. The cups are now pieces of PVC in regulation size. Flag sticks were slivers of bamboo with the numbers scribbled on paper glued

Gregarious crowd watches golf match on back yard course beside the marsh.

to them. Now the poles are short pieces of PVC with permanent triangular flags embellished with neatly-scribed hole designations.

Those sawgrass fairways are better cut now, and the sand traps are a recent addition, as are the round brass markers for the tees.

But the water hole has remained un-changed.

Jimmy greets friends with a toast.

Situated inches behind the fifth-hole green, it's an old claw-foot bathtub sunk lip-high in the ground, and it was there before the course was created.

Jim used it as a holding tank for minnows and crabs before entering the "golf business."

Jim is not only the greenskeeper but an all-round handyman and crafts person who designs and builds models of lighthouses in his spare time.

He has constructed a dandy all-purpose golf cart for the players.

The cart, built of wood and PVC, includes a rack for clubs, a holder for golf balls, drink holders (a mandatory accoutrement for this crowd), a large ash-tray filled with sand for smokers, and a slot to hold the flag at each hole while players putt out.

Jim, who's a gregarious and generous gentleman, generally

Carter displays golf awards board.

serves as caddy for all players, pulling the cart around and dutifully writing down their scores on a chalk board hanging from the cart.

Try finding a club owner who performs these duties at any other course!

Jim has spent extra time on the layout recently, prepping it for the Grand Masters Tournament culminating the summer-long grind of the island's touring non-pros.

Well, maybe you shouldn't call 'em all non-pros.

Roma, a statuesque lady who resembles Babe Dedrickson Zaharias on the course, is the reigning champ of the links, and you'd be wise not to lay any money

210

against her.

Roma, a long-time island resident, has had a virtual lock on the coveted "red ball" (a standard golf ball painted red, which designates the course champ), for what seems like forever.

She plays with it every weekend and woe be to any-one, save Roma, who tries to use it!

A regular at the Sunday outings (some say she sneaks around when no one is looking on weekdays too, putting in hours of practice time), it was Roma who coined the term Pathetic Golfer's Association.

She also invented the infamous "shovel shot" for get-ting out of deep rough. She doesn't hit the ball. She

Roma Harper checks her score card
during round at Carter's course.

shovels it out with the club head.

Play on the course isn't restricted to weekends and several islanders come to play at odd times, even when Jim and Barbara are not home. They encourage such outings, leaving the golf cart, clubs and balls in their yard for anyone who wishes to play.

The golf course was, somewhat serendipitously, Barbara's idea.

Just after moving to Tybee in 1995, she gazed at her lawn overlooking the marsh beside Horse Pen Creek and observed: "Gee, it looks like a golf course."

The next thing she knew, Jim had installed the first rudimentary layout and guests started flocking to their home for sport and conviviality.

That's typical of how the two complement one another.

Jim is a quiet fellow who grins constantly, with both pride and amusement, as his ebullient spouse regales visitors with colorful tales, many regarding the sometimes hilarious doings down at Fannie's on the Beach restaurant, where she occasionally fills in.

While clearly the more expansive of the two, Barbara sports an artistic side similar to Jim's. She makes dolls and colorful glass containers of spices and other kitchen-oriented ornaments.

In addition to the models of famous lighthouses,

some inside glass bottles, and others free-standing or encased in wood and glass boxes, Jim builds wind-chimes which clink pleasantly against the inside of bottomless bottles.

He also somehow puts things inside clear-glass lightbulbs which were once used as streetlights and mounts them on carved wood stands.

Jim does his art and craft work in a shop he set up in an old garage in Ft. Screven.

Both Barbara and Jim occasionally display and sell their creations at area craft shows and plan to open their own craft shop on the island in the near future.

"It will feature not only our work but the work of other Tybee artists," says Barbara. "There are plenty of artists and crafts people here. We don't need any-body from the outside."

"Our prices will be right," says Jim. "We're not going to rip anybody off like some of those places down on River Street."

Jim, a short, wiry man with close cropped hair, looks very much like the former U.S. Marine he is.

During a 16-month tour in Vietnam, he says he saw considerable action "out on a hill for the whole time. I got into Da Nang once or twice but that was about it."

"I was in 'Marine Corps Alley,' up around Da Nang,

and I went to Hue Phu Bai for a little while, and then Khe Sanh, where most of the Marines spent a lot of their time."

He says while "you never get over that completely and Barbara has helped me a lot," he didn't suffer through much of the post-Vietnam trauma many veterans did.

"I was pretty lucky. I fell into a pretty good job right after I got out. I don't know whether some of those guys are the way they are because they couldn't get a job or if they couldn't get a job because they are the way they are."

Barbara met Jim when they were both living and working in Jacksonville, Fla.

Jim worked for 25 years as a lineman for an electric company (that's where the light bulbs he uses in his craft work came from) and Barbara for 20 years as an insurance underwriter.

Both previously married, they became regulars in a group which gathered at the beach outside Jacksonville for weekend parties and mutual consolation concerning failed former relationships.

Jim introduced Barbara, a native of Newport, RI, to Tybee after they were married.

His family had lived in the area for several generations, owning and operating the Thunderbolt Yacht Basin for a number of years while keeping a house on Tybee, where Jim spent much of his youth surfing and hanging out on the beach.

Several years ago, he brought Barbara up to the island from Florida for a Memorial Day outing.

"I loved the place at first sight," she says. "It reminded me somehow of Newport, and I said this is where we're going to live."

With that thought in mind they formulated their retirement plans, left Jacksonville, and bought the

Jimmy enjoys the party.

house with its latent "golf course" where they now reside.

They say the course is still evolving.

"We're thinking of putting up a little clubhouse outside to hold the golf equipment and protect it from the elements," says Jim. "We may also put up floodlights."

"No, not floodlights," corrected Barbara. "It should be one of those security lights, like a streetlight,"

Jim acquiesced immediately, as usual.

The mellow Sunday golf gang all agreed that night golf would be another nice innovation on the island.

That way the party might never end.

POSTSCRIPT: *Tybee's grand old PGA golf course closed down permanently when Jim and Barbara moved away several years ago. Sad to say, it's now just another back yard.*

Sonjia Dittmar -
Popular Artist Works in a "Zoo"

Animals
And Art
Mix Well

*I*t's eclectic, perhaps somewhat eccentric, enlightening and eye catching, meshing with is proprietor like a perfect dovetail joint.

Tybee's Dragonfly Studio is owned and operated by dauntingly ebullient Sonjia Dittmar, known as Sunny to her friends because of her unceasingly sunshiny disposition.

She's petite, laughs frequently and infectiously, and glows with a natural beauty that reminds you of the younger sister you'd want if you could choose one.

Her long, golden hair is woven loosely in a single plaited ponytail. A stranger to scissors for at least eight years, it dangles to the small of her back.

Flecks of enamel and clay adorn her artist's hands and wrists like treasured jewelry.

"I don't worry about my hair or my hands," she says,

seemingly unaware of her undeniable beauty. "I just don't have the time to spend on them. Anyone who messes with their hair or fools with their hands a lot has too much time."

Sunny learned her craft during time off from her waitressing job in Atlanta before moving to Tybee 18 months ago and opening the Dragonfly Studio where she creates hand-molded clay pieces.

She specializes in primitive Native American pots - the oldest form of American pottery - and is also an expert in Japanese raku and commercial glazing, glittering with extraordinary colors.

Each of her pieces, including fish, masks, turtles, dragons, castles, and other items in addition to pots and bowls, is unique, like its creator and her studio, which rambles through several rooms in an old beach cottage, growing like topsy as her business expands.

The builder who constructed the cottage was nick-named "Half-a-Quart Jack," which Sunny surmises was because "that's what he needed each day to com-plete the project, half a quart of Jack Daniels."

She chose the name "Dragonfly" for the studio be-cause, according to myth, it represents illusion, imag-ination, and creativity, and it is those qualities which she tries to coax from clay.

Sunny designed a huge replica of a dragonfly, paint-ing it with a rainbow of colors, for the street-side sign in front of her shop. A loose-jointed mannequin leans

Sunny stands beside her Dragonfly Studio sign on Highway 80.

against the sign, and several others form a line along the fence beside the property.

Not only is the studio surprising in its seemingly unplanned meander through the cottage, but in its startling assortment of sounds and life.

Sunny is surrounded by arts and crafts in her studio.

Music permeates the premises, accompanied by the chatter of three cockatoos, four large dogs, a couple of cats and an iguana named Sinbad.

Sinbad is the reputed king of the roost. Sunny had a second such reptile named Pixie who, sad to say, passed away last winter when Sinbad refused to allow his summertime buddy to share his heating pad when the weather turned cold.

Such seems to be the nature of summer relationships at island resorts like Tybee.

Most of her miniature menagerie was "donated" by folks who no longer wanted them, according to Sunny.

Out back, a pair of turtles wander about, undisturbed by the surrounding hubbub.

Sunny has a particular affinity for turtles. She often retrieves those which have been injured by passing cars and nurses them back to health using epoxy to repair their cracked shells.

"They usually recover fine, and I release them once they are fit, but sometimes they have nerve damage and can't survive," she sighs.

With the zoo-like cacophony from the animals, the somewhat sinister masks peering ominously from the walls, the clink of clay wind chimes, and the assortment of surrealistic clay dragons squatting about, strolling through the studio is like traveling on a mystical jungle safari.

Sunny says her dragons require more time than anything else to complete and she prices them accordingly for about $800.

"I'm not planning on doing any more of those," she says. "They don't sell very well."

She believes that one thing that attracts her customers is the fact that "they're buying a one-of-a-kind thing. No two pieces are alike. Each is a new creation."

She has no molds to break because there are no molds.

Sunny is a native of the Catskill Mountain area of New York where her father worked in construction and her mother operated a restaurant. She remained

there until she was 18, developing a deep appreciation
for the various art forms produced by mountain residents.

Her family lived just outside Woodstock, and while
she embodies the quintessential spirit of such love-
ins, the famous festival occurred long before Sonjia
was old enough to participate.

Her sister, who creates graphic CD cover designs
for Atlantic Records, worked at the second Woodstock festival, but Sunny missed that one as well.

Still, she says she was always surrounded by music,
and "Upstate New York was great. All those wide-
open spaces were beautiful."

She attended Duchess Community College just outside Poughkeepsie, studying drawing and painting.
That early training continues to serve her well with
her current clay creations.

After graduation, she lived in Virginia Beach for a
while, then headed for Atlanta where she formed a
friendship with Barbara Major, a commercially successful potter who served as her instructor.

"I started out working with pottery for fun, and I'm
still doing it for fun," she smiles.

Sunny soon became infatuated with the craft and after learning the basics from her mentor, she honed her
skills through reading and by simple trial and error.

Sunny beside wall of masks in her studio.

Through extensive reading, she became acquainted with and developed a deep interest in the Japanese raku form of pottery.

"I find Japanese art and the whole Buddhist kind of thing is very relaxing," she says.

Her primitive pieces are generally black and white.

Sunny
orders her
clay in bulk
and is now
working
in red clay
with grog,
a sandy
substance
which
makes it
stronger.

She kneads
the clay
to ensure
there are
no bubbles,
then forms
animals,

Sunny flashes sunshine smile.

castles or whatever freehand and puts them aside for
a week and a half to dry in the air.

After this, she bisques them by placing them in a kiln
for about six hours to further dry and harden. The
pieces are then ready for the finishing work of glazing, smoking or "rakuing."

The smoking is done at the pit behind her studio
which is lined with sawdust and palm fronds. Exposure to the smoldering sawdust and fronds produces
the primitive black and white pieces.

The raku is glazed after being bisqued, then placed

in a propane kiln and heated to 1,200 degrees for 45 minutes, which melts the glaze.

Still hot, the raku is placed in a pile of sawdust or paper, which is ignited by the heat in a process called "reduction," which determines the final appearance, depending on whether it reduces faster or slower or wetter or dryer.

"You never know what you're going to get," says Sunny. "The pieces, in effect, create themselves."

A third method she uses is "commercial glazing," in which the glaze is applied immediately after the bisquing process, before being put back into the kiln to set the surface.

When Sonjia first arrived in the Savannah area, she placed several pieces in the River Street Gallery and created an unusual set of wine carafes for Tybee's North Beach Grill.

Her gallery pieces sold well, and her reputation grew to the point where she had trouble keeping up with her sales and trying to maintain an inventory.

When the Tybee cottage became available, she and her husband, Steven, purchased it immediately. Now the studio is not only where she works but the only location in which she displays and sells her pottery.

Sunny's reputation has grown to the point that she is frequently called upon to conduct classes and seminars.

She is particularly fond of teaching children and plans to initiate six-week classes year-round for youngsters in her studio starting this summer.

"All children need to be exposed to art to enhance their creativity," she says.

Asked to discuss her future aspirations, Sunny says she's simply going to continue doing what she's doing.

"I'm not a real planner," she confesses. "So far, things have been going great, and I'm just going to keep at it."

"I love Tybee," she says enthusiastically. "The people really make this place, and I like the solitude. This is a great place to be."

Those who know her feel Tybee is blessed by the presence of this ever-ebullient island treasure.

POSTSCRIPT: Despite her avowed love of the island, Sonjia Dittmar sold her studio and departed Tybee not long after this was written. She moved to Asheville, N.C., where she is reportedly continuing to produce her art.

Walter Parker -
Popular Mayor Unopposed, Unafraid

Claims Promotion, Travel Are Just Part of the Job

Folks must either love this guy or think he's unbeatable.

Tybee Mayor Walter Parker is running unopposed in the upcoming November election marking the first time in recent memory a mayoral candidate on the island has been handed victory in advance.

The mayor's record is proof of his impressive popularity.

His next term will mark his third consecutive and sixth overall two-year term as mayor beginning in 1985 after serving a term on City Council in the early 1970s.

Though a guaranteed shoo in, the mayor - unlike some folks who would hunker down and avoid the issues until the votes are counted - is not afraid to confront either critics or controversial topics.

Parker says the most frequently voiced criticism against him is his reputation for travel and his image as a promoter, rather than a hardnosed administrator.

"Promotion is extremely important for the island," he says. "Telling people about Tybee and getting them to come here helps the island. It's good for everybody."

"I can do the job of an administrator, I have in the past when that was necessary, but with a city manager that's a lot less important now. It's his job to handle the city's administrative affairs while reporting to City Council."

"Public relations and lobbying is a major portion and I think one of the most important parts of my job. The lobbying effort is crucial at the state and national level. It makes a big difference, and those people will let you know that."

As for travel, he says:

"I do travel a lot. It may not make me the best mayor, but it certainly makes me a more informed mayor and helps me make decisions, and I think that's important."

"I don't spend the city's money frivolously. I'm very conservative when I travel, and I try to get whichever organization I'm going to meet with to pay for my fares and meals, and a lot of the time they do."

The mayor said he considers travel one of the best

things about his job because "you get a chance to meet some of the most interesting people in the world, and you get a chance to really learn some things about what's going on in other communities and how you may be able to apply that."

Two of the lobbying efforts on which he has spent considerable time with commendable results are beach renourishment and the development of Hutchinson Island.

Mayor Parker at ease in Tybee's City Hall.

The trade center and golf course on Hutchinson will be very important to Tybee, he says.

"I just attended a meeting in Savannah about it, and they gave me some numbers. It's going to be very impressive. That's one reason we donated one percent of our hotel/motel tax to the operating expenses."

"Those people are going to spill over here. There's no doubt in my mind that we're going to benefit big time! People who go to the conventions have families that can go to the beach and enjoy it. It's going to be good for us."

As for beach renourishment, the third separate project for which will begin later this year, Parker claims it is a requisite for the island.

"You have to have a decent beach not only for the tourists - a big factor in our economic wellbeing, but for the residents, and it's a factor in protecting us from hurricanes," he says.

"That is important. Two storms hit in North Carolina a couple of years ago. One hit a beach where there was no renourishment, and almost every building there was destroyed. Adjoining it was a beach that had been renourished two years before, and there was just minor damage to a couple of buildings. That proves its value in protecting the island."

Parker has been intimately involved in every renourishment, beginning with the first in the 1970s, and nobody has worked harder at jawboning legislators to get state and federal funding for such projects.

His next goal for the shore is to convince officials that sand from the planned dredging of the Savannah River channel should be pumped onto Tybee's beach, which experts say could add 100 yards to its width, perhaps at no cost to the city.

If this plan is successful, it may mean erosion can be controlled for years, eliminating the need for future cycles of costly renourishment.

"Every study I've ever seen shows that a deep channel to the north of a beach prevents natural renourishment with sand moving down from other beaches to the north," says Parker.

"The Savannah River channel is responsible for interrupting the flow of this sand and the continued erosion of our beach. It's only fair that they should give us the sand they have taken away."

He also weighs in on controversial subjects such as building setbacks, condominiums, taxes and the proposed construction of a gymnasium and pool complex.

The mayor believes Tybee residents "basically want to have an island and a community that they feel comfortable in, with good services where they can raise their children and not have to worry."

"What happens in the commercial area I don't think bothers the majority of the residents. They're con-

*Parker displays omni-present smile at ballgame
in Jaycee Park.*

cerned if there's over-development in a neighborhood,
which I can well understand."

"I think we have some ordinances in place and once
the C-2 is set, we'll be pretty much covered and not

have anything that's going to impact the people."

That C-2 area along Highway 80 does cause him some concern, however.

"I don't think we have to restrict it so much that there's not going to be any building along there because it is a highway, and I think it needs to be looked at and studied carefully," he said.

"We need to see what size lots are available and what needs to be done. We need to encourage as much commercial development as we can because as Tybee grows more and more people are coming down and they need services and that is the basis of keeping our tax base low."

Of the condominiums directly across from City Hall which have sparked adverse reaction from residents because of their design and proximity to the street, Parker says:

"It could have been done much better and I'm glad the zoning laws were changed to prevent something like that."

"It doesn't need to be that close to the street. It could have been set back... just to come and see that detracts from the overall ambiance of Tybee, and we don't want to see that."

The mayor said he is not pleased with "the mass along Strand Avenue but that's a very small area.

"We have a few spots where you have these big buildings, but overall Tybee has maintained its flavor over the years in large part because we've held the 35-foot height limit and we've found that there are a lot of people who are history buffs and buy these old houses and restore them."

"You can see what's happened down in front of Officers Row. Those houses are built to resemble old beach houses, and I think we're going to maintain that flavor on Tybee for the foreseeable future."

Addressing the issue of burgeoning property taxes, Parker said "I'm in the same boat" with other islanders who are chagrined by their rapid rise.

"I hate to see that money go out in taxes, but Tybee has only a six mil tax base where you're paying 11.5 mils to the county and 22 mils to the school board."

"In comparison, Tybee's doing pretty well trying to provide the services we're providing to the people and keeping that tax base low."

"It's a fine balance there. We certainly want to protect the citizens and especially those on fixed incomes. Tybee does have a provision that if you're under $30,000 in income and 62 years or older your taxes will not go up no matter what the assessment is."

Parker said he has reservations about both the timing of building the long-planned new gymnasium and pool complex and its proposed location in Memorial Park.

"I think there are some options we can still look at," he says.

"This (Memorial Park) seems like an ideal spot for a facility like that, but it will take up so much space. It will require parking, and I hate to see the park gobbled up by a facility like that. It would take a big area."

"I'm not opposed to the idea of a gym and pool, but I think it's premature. I know a lot of people are going to disagree with that, but I think we should study our financial situation a little closer."

"We're depending on the revenue from the antenna rental on our water tanks, and I don't know how long that's going to go on. Maybe in two, three or five years those things are going to be obsolete. They're going to have satellites or other things, and they're not going to need those antennas."

"We have to think about a gym and pool being very expensive to operate and maintain. It's going to cost the city a lot of money to have a facility like that."

"If we can work those numbers and it seems to be okay, that's fine… if the people really do want it but I don't know how many of the people really want it."

Parker says he had hoped to have the question of the gym included on a referendum in the election, but the city attorney said it would not be possible for legal reasons.

"I'd still like to see something, even if it's just a piece of paper in the back of the voting areas to let people say yes or no to the gymnasium," he says.

"I would like to know how the people of the island feel as a whole. I think their feelings should be known and I think they should be educated to the facts before we ask that question."

Parker said when the gym fund was first started the original site suggested was on city-owned property near the police station "and that was a logical thing."

The mayor relaxes and smiles frequently when he recalls growing up on Tybee and the somewhat circuitous path which led to his current seat of power.

Just after his birth in Screven County, his family moved to Savannah where his stepfather operated a service station.

Parker was 9 when they moved into a house on Tybee's Officers Row in 1947.

He remembers the old Ft. Screven Officers Club was still standing and Lukey Boyer, owner of Boyer Motors in Savannah, lived next door.

"I grew up on Tybee," he says. "I went to the island school and then commuted back to Washington Avenue and Savannah High School."

That ride into the city on the school bus was memorable for its minor mishaps.

Mayor Parker with long-time Councilman Jack Youmans.

"It was bus No. 66, and it was all banged up on the right side," he laughs. "It hit the bridge quite often."

Back in those days there seemed to be an endless number of things for a boy to do "even though my family didn't have a lot of money and I went to work when I was 11," he says.

"In the summertime there was a lot more activity on the (beach) front. The pier and pavilion were there, and there was skating on the Pavilion, and the bowling alley and all sorts of amusements were down there."

"In the winter the restaurants and everything shut down. There was very little open on the beach, but the kids always got together to have parties from the time we were about 10 to 16."

"There was always somebody's house you went to as a group on weekends. I don't know whether that's happening now as much as it was."

"And we used to have movies in the old theater!"

Parker remembers seeing a much ballyhooed and, for the times, very risqué film starring voluptuous Jane Russell at the old theater.

"I remember I saw *The Outlaw* there," he laughs. "I was just a kid, but I sat through it twice! We also had movies at the old fire station at Ft. Screven in the building where they hold kick boxing classes now."

In those days Parker says the government did very little to provide entertainment "but there was no need for it. Everybody seemed to have a good time. Now we've got the Y here with all sorts of activities."

"But lifestyles change. People change. There was no television back then, and you had to entertain yourself and entertain each other."

238

"Families were much closer back then, and then times changed with mothers and fathers working."

"Now I can see that pendulum coming back around."

"You see more parents getting more involved, especially with their kids at the Y and things, which I think is good. I don't know what's caused it. Maybe they're just seeing there was a problem and are trying to rectify that."

After graduating from high school, Parker studied engineering at Virginia Polytechnic Institute, beginning as a co-op student in its Norfolk, Va. division prior to heading to the main campus in Blacksburg, Va., alternating quarters working at Glenn L. Martin Co. in Baltimore, then attending classes.

Knowing he was about to be drafted as he entered his senior year in 1957 ("I was not at the top of my class," he admits), Parker volunteered for the Army Security Agency, serving in Germany for two years.

Following his discharge, he took a position with the National Security Agency in Washington, D.C., returning only briefly to Savannah to marry his wife, Mary Ann, who he had known for years.

They remained in Washington until he resigned his position when he was scheduled for service overseas in 1967.

Fortuitously, his stepfather, William Reynolds, asked him to join the expanding family business on Tybee.

The family had operated Bill's Grill for some time and ultimately expanded their holdings to include The Corner (a snack bar in Christy's), an ice cream shop around the corner on what was then 16th Street, Reynold's Apartments, and The Heritage rental apartments.

"If I knew then how things were going to develop, I'd have kept it all and maybe bought more," he laughs.

"It's unbelievable how Tybee has grown, but overall, I think it's been good for the island and certainly good for the economy."

Looking back, the mayor says he has "been in the concession business a long time."

That activity continues occasionally even today in conjunction with a friend who worked with him at the National Security Agency.

The friend operates food concessions at fairs and other gatherings and sometimes asks Parker to join him at various locations when his regular purveyor of ice cream is not available.

"Every once in a while I go out with him and help him sell ice cream," says Parker.

"It's not just anybody who can operate those machines. It's soft ice cream but its real. It's not ice milk or anything like that."

"It takes experience to get the formula right and operate it economically and it's fun to do that occasionally, but it calls for 14-hour days and that's getting a little harder on this old man."

Shortly after he entered the family business, Parker became involved in the island's community activities, joining the Optimist Club under the sponsorship of T.S. Chu.

He was the youngest member of that club for his initial five years and ultimately became its president.

Being the youngest member had some shortcomings.

"I think the average age for members at that time was about 70," he laughs, "but they were some mighty nice people."

"I remember when you joined you were supposed to call everybody by their first names, and the members were older, and I was used to saying mister."

"It was kind of hard for me to call somebody like Mr. Chu 'T.S.' or whatever. They'd fine you a dollar when you didn't use a first name. I got fined lots of times."

Parker was also president of the island's Chamber of Commerce and served a term on City Council in 1973-74, but opted not to run again until he sought the position of mayor in 1985 "because I was just too busy."

He says he got his start at elective office by serving as secretary of his graduating class in high school.

Mayor Walter Parker outside city hall.

The most difficult part of being mayor is "the time it takes to get things done," he says. "Unfortunately, the wheels of government roll very slowly."

"It's like this beach renourishment project. We worked over three years to get it, but it's over $9 million, and that's substantial for an island this size."

"I worked with the committee that was appointed by the governor for five years before we got the Coastal Zone Management Act in place through the state legislature."

"It's a long, drawn-out process to try to get these things done. That's why it's important to maintain consistency."

"I know a lot of people say there should be term limits but if they are too severe you run into the fact that you don't have continuity and you lose the momentum you build trying to get something accomplished for your municipality."

Parker believes two years is too short a term and "we ought to look at that again."

"I think Pooler is the only other municipality in the area that has two-year terms. We should have four-year terms. It makes it much easier to operate and do things."

The mayor says he has been "accused of voting for my friends and against my friends or whatever, but I've really tried to look at the situation, and I don't let personalities affect me."

"I get advice from a lot of people on this island and
that's fine. I like it. I want to hear from the people,
but I have to look at the overall picture and make a
decision."

"It doesn't reflect on who's for or who's against. I try
to make that decision for the best for the island as a
whole."

"But you never know if you're making the right decision. You just do the best you can at the time and
hope that it's right. I think the majority of the time
it has been right."

As to Tybee's future, the mayor says he doesn't vi-
sualize much change in the commercial area because
"that's pretty much set right now, but there'll be
some."

"I think you'll see more and more houses on the island. I think you will see more and more duplexes
just because of the land value."

"I think you're going to see a younger group, and
they're going to build a duplex and live in one side
and rent the other. I think economics is going to
demand that, and that's not bad because we have a
great deal of our island zoned R-2 that's available to
them."

He also expects an influx of affluent people retiring
to Tybee, some of whom have had family homes for

years that they will renovate and make year-round homes.

Of the current city council, Parker says "overall, they've done a good job, but this council has not come together as well as some of the other councils I have dealt with, but these people who are on there now are as sincere as any group I have ever seen. They want to do the right thing and they work towards that. We have some bright people."

"We've had some controversy, but I think we've made some progress."

He's enthusiastic about the upcoming election because "I think we have a chance this time to get a very good council. We have a chance to get some real cooperation."

Parker says the relatively clear-cut differences between groups of candidates this year will be a good opportunity for voters to let officials know what they want for the island and "that's important."

Asked about his own platform, the mayor chuckled as he responded: "I'm running on my past record."

Judging from his repeated success at the ballot box that appears to be more than sufficient.

POSTSCRIPT: Walter Parker served as mayor of Tybee Island for 16 years until he was finally defeated in the 2005 election, after which he and

Mary Ann moved to Bloomingdale to be closer to their daughter and her family. As a tribute to the mayor and his lengthy and outstanding service, the island's ocean-front pier was re-named the Walter Parker Pavilion and Pier in 2007. The gymnasium he discussed was built in Memorial Park, but not the pool, which is still a subject of discussion. That duplex boom and influx of permanent residents he predicted never materialized, having been supplanted by a growing number of absentee owners of short-term rentals, which has become a current political hot potato. Walter Parker passed away on Sept. 17, 2023, following a brief illness.

Peter Bannon -

Island Neighbor in Your Living Room

Newsman
Finds Home
On Tybee

*H*e's in your living room every evening, bringing in a little class with his conservative suits and ties and sometimes solemn demeanor.

Still, there's a bit of a homey quality about him, like maybe he could be a neighbor from down the street.

If you live on Tybee, the neighbor part is true. So is the homey part when he's away from the office.

He's Peter Bannon, news anchor for WSAV-TV in Savannah and one of the favorite sources of news for many area residents, at least those who can get clear reception on Channel 3.

Peter's been anchoring the news on that channel for just over a year.

He and his effervescent wife, Theresa, have been anchoring the social scene on the island somewhat longer. Both have visited the island frequently for 20 years and Theresa spent summer school vacations at her family's luxurious old home on Officers Row in Ft. Screven.

It was Theresa who introduced Peter to the island when they were college students, he at Notre Dame, she at nearby St. Mary's.

"It (Tybee) was probably why we fell in love," laughs Theresa. "We had this wonderful summer with the starry skies and the moon down here while we were in school. It probably had nothing to do with us. It was the island."

They both get a pleasant glow when they recall that first phase of a romance that clearly continues, just like their love of the beach.

Peter, having just enrolled in Notre Dame, was intent on

Peter Bannon covers St. Patrick's Day parade in Savannah.

248

his studies and was seriously considering training to become a Jesuit priest at the time.

That's when he helped a friend carry her luggage into St. Mary's (which Notre Dame students referred to as "the wife farm") and met Theresa.

That changed everything.

Born in Brooklyn, he not only became inextricably hooked on Theresa but on the island as well once she introduced him to it.

"Actually, most people here think I'm the one from the South and she's from New York," Peter says, grinning at his wife.

They're both into biking, fishing, sea air and late-night excursions to Doc's Bar and other island venues. Occasionally, they'll lead revelers back to their home on the north end once the commercial bistros close.

"Where else would you want to be?" asks Peter of his move to Tybee.
But the route back to Tybee following his college romance with the island was circuitous.

Peter joined the Marine Corps when he was just out of college and was serving in Vietnam when his son was born. The boy was nine months old when he first saw him.

Peter's initial television experience came in Atlanta

in 1970, when, just after being discharged from the service, he took a job with the Georgia Educational Television Network as a cameraman, technical director and writer/producer, among other things.

"I really wanted to be a writer," says Peter. "That was my first real love. But the money was in front of the camera."

He joined WAGA-TV in Atlanta in 1971, starting out as a cameraman and then becoming a news producer, director, and the anchor of several news programs.

Peter says he still gets along well with camera crews because of his own early experience.

"I think like they do," he says. "We communicate and I don't waste their time having them shoot everything in sight."

His timing in Atlanta was fortuitous.

"It was a magic time in Atlanta then," Peter says. "The civil rights movement was still hot, and the place had a really high presence. A lot of people moved on to New York from there."

After four years, Peter got the big city bug as well and headed north.

He worked in New York for eight years on WABC-TV's Eyewitness News ("Joan Lunden and I were hired on the same day," he recalls. "We were dubbed Ken and Barbie.") as anchor on morning newscasts,

correspon-
dent, and
music editor.

"That was a
magic time in
television," he
says. "I was
very lucky to
be there at
that time with
Eyewitness
News which
was a seminal
influence on
what news is
today."

"It was a real
cowboy outfit.
On air people

Peter is dressed for business.

really ruled that place. I remember Geraldo (Rivera)
coming in one day and throwing a general manager
out of his chair, onto the floor. That doesn't happen
anymore."

Peter says he was surprised to find that New York
lagged behind Atlanta in live television coverage in
the mid-1970s, and that led to one of his more embarrassing experiences.

"They were pushing shark meat at the time as the
'other white meat' and were doing a promotion at
a fish market," recalls Peter. "There was a guy out

there barbecuing the stuff on a grill, and I was doing a live cut of him."

"He handed me a piece, and they hadn't taken care of that shark at all. It was really foul and there's nothing worse than putting bad fish on a grill."

"I said OK, I'm ready. I'll eat any kind of fish. And I put this stuff in my mouth, and I spit it out. I didn't vomit because I had a dry stomach, but I was heaving right there on camera."

"I said get off me, I'm dying! I'm really dying! Call 911! Get someone to help me!"

"The guy gave me a great big glass of beer to wash the taste out, and they stayed right with me on camera for about three minutes. It was a disaster!"

Another time Peter was assigned to do a rainy Labor Day traffic piece to capture the exodus from the city.

The problem was there was no traffic at his location, and each time they put him on the air there was nothing to show except Peter getting drenched. After several passes, the entire news team started laughing each time they went to Peter.

"Finally, I just started doing a really horrible version of Gene Kelly's *Singing in the Rain*, dancing around for two and a half minutes while the rain poured down," laughs Peter. "The show became famous as my *Singing in the Rain* routine."

But New York was also the scene of one of his most impressive newscasts, his Emmy-winning coverage of the death of John Lennon.

Peter was in a studio only three blocks from the shooting and dashed to the scene with a camera crew on a hunch "because shootings don't usually happen on 72nd Street in New York."

He and the crew arrived while Yoko Ono was still on the sidewalk and Lennon was being placed in an ambulance. As soon as a backup crew appeared, Peter ran to Roosevelt Hospital two blocks away.

By happenstance, his station's afternoon news producer was also in the hospital, having just been injured in a biking accident, and he was lying on a gurney next to Lennon.

Peter was on the air live constantly over the next 12 hours interviewing hundreds of people who converged on the hospital once news of Lennon's death was announced through his feed during the Monday Night Football program.

Peter is out for an evening on Tybee.

"It was like a sea of people flowing down the streets toward the hospital, all moving quietly," recalls Peter, who says even the hardened newsmen gathered at the hospital uttered an audible sigh when news of Lennon's death was officially announced.

But the frenzied pace of the Big Apple eventually took its toll on Peter.

He says he knew it was time to move on when he was covering the report of a little girl lost in the Christmas shopping crunch at Macy's.

"We're pushing this story about this lost kid, a typical New York story, and we're going to find the girl and get her back to her parents and all that stuff when I get a tip from homicide to get up to the Bronx over near the George Washington Bridge."

"What the story was is that the common-law husband had beaten a child to death, dismembered it, and was trying to burn the pieces in a 55-gallon oil drum out in front of this derelict building."

"I just stood there and thought people don't really need to know this. It's going to sicken everyone, and it isn't going to do me a whole lot of good. That's when we decided that maybe we'd go back to Atlanta and try a little something different."

Peter again joined WAGA-TV, then moved on to WSB-TV to anchor weekend newscasts and do general assignment reporting.

"I always liked reporting," he says. "It always felt like a public service, and we got paid pretty well to do it. And I really enjoy telling the people what's going on as long as it was useful information. One more dead body in the street is trivia. I don't mean to diminish that life, but it's trivial information."

"Why do they do cop stories? Because it's easy. It's one-stop shopping. You've got your pros and your cons, and you've got your whole story. Hopefully, somebody's still running around with a gun out and you've got everything. It's a commodity. If you do a story about property taxes, it's a lot more complicated."

"There used to be great story tellers and cameramen, classy guys. What they tend to do now is all the cosmetic stuff, gilding the lily, packaging the stuff. The actual content is not that good. I still wince when I see some of this stuff."

"I like to see it nice and clean, simple and ele-

Peter chats with Wanda Parker, owner of Doc's Bar on Tybee.

gant. It's the difference in the economy of a swing between a golf pro and a hacker. Keeping it simple and comprehensible. That's the challenge."

"There's an added degree of difficulty for television news. It's a straight line. They only get it once, and you've got to assume you've got the viewer's attention. It's like a thread. If you lose 'em, if at any point in the story they get confused, there's no way for them to go back and get it right."

"Some of the (television) people get it and some of 'em don't."

In 1991, Peter decided to go out on his own and started Seajen Productions, a media services company whose clients included Bell South, The Discovery Channel, and the Billy Graham Evangelical Assn.

That might have continued but for the loss of his 20-year-old son, a college student, in an automobile accident.

His son's death was not the only family tragedy at that time.

"During a two-and-a-half-year period we lost our son, my mother, my father and Theresa's father," said Peter. "It was like shell shock. We were just living kind of stunned."

Finally, they decided to take stock and decide what they really wanted to do.

Their conclusion?

Tybee was where they wanted to be and "since I'm kind of a one-act pony, a return to television broadcasting in a smaller market outside the big city where we could be closer as a family was what I wanted."

Just two weeks after that discussion, a relative faxed Peter a copy of a story saying the former news anchor at WSAV was leaving.

"And that's how we got here," he says. "It was like one of those Divine coincidence things, the way it worked out."

His biggest problem in landing the job was to convince the station owners that someone with his level of experience was committed to stay in Savannah.

Peter couldn't understand their disbelief.

"My son's ashes are spread in the sea off Tybee," he said. "This is my home."

Peter enjoys a day off on the water.

Theresa Bannon at picnic in the park.

And there was never a question for Peter about living in the city.

"Why would you live in Savannah when the ocean is just 12 miles away?" he asks.

Most mornings you'll now find Peter and Theresa out behind the Marlin Marina fishing for flounder. Both agree that Theresa is more successful at catching them.

"I'm more technical about it," said Peter, casting his lure from the dock after rigging his wife's line for her recently. "Besides, sometimes I feel the fish just get in the way. To me this is such a privilege just to be here."

Or you might spot them touring the island on their bicycles.

It's not that conservative, neatly dressed TV persona you'll see, however.

Peter's usually wearing multi-pocketed khaki trousers with an open-necked shirt, and he's smiling broadly as the wind leaves his normally perfectly combed blond TV hair in disarray.

The two of them, cute, bubbly, diminutive Theresa, and Peter, looking like a carefree, sun-bleached beach boy, seem inseparable.

Most nights you'll find them down at Doc's, with Peter singing or keeping time to the music with a variety of percussion instruments while Theresa watches the scene, smiling demurely from a seat in a corner, deftly fending off occasional unwanted advances from newcomers who don't know Peter's her man.

The instruments, which include assorted jars containing dried corn, are available to anyone who wants to join in, and they're Peter's own innovation.

"The idea came from the musical sessions we used to have at our house in Ridgewood, N.J., just outside New York, when I worked there," he says.

Peter played guitar and the piano and was joined by a group of music-loving friends who enjoyed playing together.

"But we didn't want one of those typical sessions where the wives sat together in one room and the kids were upstairs watching TV while the men played," he said.

They brought them all together as participants by passing out jars of dried rice and other makeshift instruments so everyone who was not playing a regular instrument could join in as the rhythm section.

"It really worked," he says. "Some of it sounded really good. We thought about maybe doing a recording or booking ourselves somewhere, but some of the people were afraid to appear in public."

That doesn't seem to bother the late-night group at Tybee's south end. Dozens grab a bottle of corn, a bongo or a tambourine and joyfully keep time to the music, with Peter leading the pack.

You can expect to find him in your home, right there in the living room on the TV for a long time to come.

"I can't see myself being any other place," says Peter, when asked about his future aspirations. "Where else would you want to be?"

POSTSCRIPT: Peter Bannon retired not long after this was written, but just as he promised, he remained on Tybee. Peter passed away in 2022. Theresa still resides in their big house on Officers Row. On most Mondays you'll find her stretching her legs walking from her home to the popular Farmer's Market on the historic Tybee Lighthouse grounds several blocks away.

Zoe Randall -
New York Lady Settles in South

Big City Pace
Slows Down
To Tybee Time

*S*he's a Big Apple lady with a glorious halo of Red Delicious hair.

Zoe (pronounced Zo-E) Randall has been in the Savannah area for two years now, but her speech and demeanor remain those of a fast-track trotting New York woman.

One of the few concessions she's made to our languid southern setting is the weekends she spends lolling about Tybee aboard "Trixie," a houseboat she and her husband, Tom, recently acquired.

The name "Trixie," incidentally, came with the boat.

"We hated it at first and were going to change it," says Zoe. "But it's a tacky little thing and the name just seemed to fit."

The funky little craft fits perfectly on Tybee where it is moored at MarLin Marina, allowing the couple

*Zoe and husband Tom aboard houseboat docked
at Tybee marina.*

to relax to the sounds of jazz wafting out from the
marina restaurant where Harvey Ray plays a cool
saxophone on weekends.

Harvey is also an expatriate New Yorker who once
played with the likes of Gerry Mulligan and Lionel
Hampton.

Zoe, who spent years in an inner circle of big-city jazz
aficionados and performers, developed a close camaraderie with Harvey and has enticed him to perform in
one of her latest ventures, a multi-media performance
entitled "Midsummer Jazz," which will open at 8 p.m.
tomorrow (Friday, July 25) at The Gallery Espresso
in Savannah.

This jazz "happening" incorporates literary, musical,
and visual art forms. Zoe is the director and writer

and will be one of the performing artists.

It is being presented by The City of Savannah Department of Cultural Affairs/Leisure Services Bureau and is supported in part by the Georgia Council for the Arts through appropriations from the Georgia General Assembly.

The show is open to the public, free of charge.

Visual artist and native Savannahian Carmela Aliffi and poet, literary critic and performance artist Tom Lavazzi will also perform in "Midsummer Jazz," a celebration of jazz in a multi-media exposition uniting the mediums of literature, music, and visual art.

Related artwork utilized in the performance, including text, music, and paintings, will remain on exhibit until Aug. 8.

Zoe, an extraordinarily high energy lady with a delectably lithe body and a temperament as feisty as her fiery red hair, is currently involved in a number of literary projects.

She recently won a City Lights Theater one-act play competition.

Her play, along with those of two other winners, will be performed at the theater two weekends next month (Aug. 15-17 and Aug. 22-24).

Members of the audience will vote on each play to determine which of the three is their favorite.

Zoe teaches English at Savannah State University; conducts fiction seminars at The Coastal Georgia Center in Savannah and is a staff writer and public-relations person for the newly formed performance art group "TEZ" (techno eschatological zippers).

"I love being in the classroom and teaching," she says, "but I'd really prefer to be teaching creative writing. I love to write."

And writing she is.

She is cranking out short stories and working on "Water Play," a memoir she hopes to publish in the near future.

But a novel she had been writing for some time has been pushed to the back burner.

With the working title "Going Home," it's the tale of a drama teacher's extended affair with a married man who lives on a houseboat while his wife stays in the city. The teacher inherits the houseboat when the man dies.

Zoe says the story is loosely based on an old love affair, but when the romance ended she was disinclined to continue her work despite the fact that she had received encouraging feedback from prospective publishers.

Zoe has published creative and cultural/theoretical pieces in magazines in New York, Pennsylvania and Canada and has presented her work at a number of conferences, most recently in Savannah at the 25th anniversary meeting of The Popular Culture Assn. in the South and The American Culture Assn. in the South.

She holds a master's degree in English Literature from Hunter College and was elected to Phi Beta Kappa in 1994.

Zoe has had what seems a somewhat serendipitous affair with life since her birth in Bridgeport, Conn.

Her father was a salesman, and the family moved about the country until her parents' divorce, following which she and her mother lived with Zoe's grandparents in a Bridgeport suburb.

When her mother remarried, they moved to New Jersey, where Zoe completed high school.

She claims she was always in quest of "something" which, until recently, was invariably in a big city ("farm girl" never enters your mind when conversing with this erudite lady who espouses precise, slightly strident enunciation), Zoe entered and dropped out of several colleges.

"I wrote a lot of bad poetry and drank a lot of bad wine" back then, she recalls.

One day, while still a teenager, she was involved in a traffic accident while driving into New York City, and "I totaled my car," she says.

But rather than having the car repaired or replaced, Zoe used the insurance money to rent a small studio apartment.

"I wanted to live in the big city, and I wanted to write," she explains of that decision.

What she did then was become deeply involved in the study of macrobiotics, pen a lot of poetry, and go to work for a limousine service.

That company's affluent owner took Zoe under her wing, teaching her about good food, the good life, and toney places in the big city.

"She took me to the best restaurants and flew me out to The Hamptons," says Zoe.

Such exposure resulted in a shift in goals for what was then a highly impressionable young lady.

"I thought maybe I ought to marry money and I went through that for a little while but it was very boring," Zoe recalls.

Then she met David Berger, a jazz musician and arranger who was conducting an orchestra at Lincoln Center and had just completed work on the popular musical "The Best Little Whorehouse in Texas."

They met in a bar where Berger had gone to hear a blues singer.

"I was very taken with him," says Zoe. "He was a

musician and arranger and seemed to be quite successful."

"He was arrogant as hell, still is, and I had a kind of
inferiority complex," she laughs.

"He's a man who doesn't tolerate any kind of mediocrity at all. I stopped wearing polyester and sold all
my bad rock and roll records and started drinking
good wines. And I started becoming educated - I'd
always been a fan - about jazz music."

Zoe indicates she was surprised to learn that "he
loved me, and since he hated any kind of mediocrity,
I started thinking that maybe I was kind of special."

What Berger didn't love was her poetry.

"He hated it, so I threw it all away," says Zoe.

That's when she realigned her personal goals once
more.

"I decided we'd get married, and I'd have a boy and a
girl and a shaggy dog and a Volvo station wagon and
this neat New York City lifestyle I'd never had the
option of having before," she smiles.

After her marriage, Zoe occupied the time she formerly spent writing bad poetry designing good sweaters
and selling her designs to magazines, including *Family Circle*, *Vogue*, *McCall's* and *Knitting*.

She also worked in an exclusive yarn store on Madi-

Zoe Randall relaxes on Tybee.

son Avenue for a while and studied the *Prophecies of Nostradamus.*

Zoe says she considered moving to New Zealand to raise sheep based on that prognosticator's prediction that "New York would be blown off the face of the map," but changed her mind when Third World nations took over the lion's share of the sheep business using less expensive labor.

Zoe had the boy and the girl, Caleb and Kate, but never got the Volvo "and I became dissatisfied," she says. "It just didn't work out."

Far more than the vehicle was apparently missing.

She says she was delighted that marriage enabled her to meet and become friends with many of the country's most famous jazz musicians, but that just wasn't enough.

"I told David I was unhappy," she says. "Then I started rebelling and going to foreign films and old art deco cafes and listening to Edith Piaf.

"When I told him I wanted a divorce, he suggested I go back to school, and I thought, God, what a generous man. What he was really saying was maybe you'll wise up and see what you have."

Turns out, he was wrong, at least from his perspective.

Zoe returned to school alright. She attended Hunter

College, where she obtained both her undergraduate and graduate degrees and became an adjunct professor.

While at Hunter she also got her divorce, after what she describes as "a very bitter, *War of the Roses* kind of battle."

It was also at Hunter that she met her present husband, Tom, who was a part-time teacher there. They met while he was sitting at a computer adjacent to hers and had difficulty searching for material in connection with his research.

"I made a suggestion and then pressed his reset button for him and that was it!" laughs Zoe.

They quickly established that they both taught English at Hunter - he days, she nights - and shared a deep mutual interest in literature and music.

But their initial relationship was not Utopian.

Zoe dated both Tom and another man simultaneously for a while before weighing the two affairs, breaking up with Tom, and moving in with his competitor.

"Those were 13 of the most miserable days of my life," she says of her brief fling.

Fortuitously, Tom called shortly after she terminated her unhappy soiree to ask if she would collaborate with him on a performance art piece called *Niagara on the Rocks*.

"We were always good friends, and when we started working together, we just picked up where we left off," smiles Zoe.

They've been together ever since.

When Tom received the offer of a tenure track teaching position at Savannah State College, Zoe followed, despite the fact that she had just been accepted by Columbia University for work on her Ph.D.

They performed their collaborative art piece at Savannah's City Lights Theater last year.

Residing here was her initial exposure to "southern living," and Zoe says she's found the experience "mostly delightful."

"I love the sky. I love the green. I love the lowlands. I love the water," she says enthusiastically.

"I find myself walking slower, and that's good. I'm a little high strung, and it's good for me to be in a slower place."

"But if I'm at a service station and I just want to pay for my gas or buy a bottle of water and I really want to get someplace in a hurry, well, okay, I know I just have to deal with it, otherwise I'll look like a pushy New York woman, and I don't want to give the North a bad name by living up to the stories."

"And I hate the bugs, and this is a heat I have never known before (it was 99 degrees on Tybee, with a heat index of 110, the afternoon we chatted).

"I really like the people, but I've found some are a little wary of me. I do feel different because I'm a woman from New York City. I just feel different."

"A principal at my daughter's school told me 'Yall never live down that New York thing.' That was the way she put it, and I kind of feel that way."

Zoe and her shaggy dog.

What bothers Zoe most, however, is the same thing that bothers most of us.

"It's sitting in a traffic jam at Abercorn and DeRenne," she says. "If I'm going to be in traffic and I'm going to be aggravated, I want to be in New York City."

Still, the only time she hits her horn is "when somebody pulls out directly in front of me when I'm doing 55 miles an hour. I tap on the horn, and then they look at me like I'm the jerk!"

She says she's startled on her trips back to New York now when the driver behind her blows his horn the instant a traffic light turns green.

"Now I look back and say shut up," she laughs.

Zoe admits, with obvious satisfaction, that she'll never be mistaken for a "Southern Belle."

She says she conformed in many ways to the lives of her two spouses, "but I'm now at a point in my life and in my writing career and my aesthetic sense that I want very much to keep my sense of who I am. It's important to me."

For now, the South looks pretty good to her as she reflects: "I had a very exciting life in New York, but I wasn't happy. I had a miserable marriage, and I don't anymore."

She and Tom are now planning to move out to Tybee.

And Zoe's finally got her shaggy dog, a gentle, mixed-breed with loving, doe-like eyes that follow Zoe's every move.

And to top it off, Tom gave her that long-awaited Volvo.

It seems a marriage made in Heaven, in a place most of us feel is pretty close.

POSTSCRIPT: *Zoe Randall says she roamed a bit before returning to Savannah where she now intends to stay. She says she's is still with Tom because "good men are impossible to ditch."*

Georges Spriggs & Jackson -
Partners Meet After Close Calls

Two Georges Cook Up Success on Tybee

*I*t must be fate, by George.

Make that fate by Georges.

There are two of 'em, Georges, that is, but that's just a small part of the coincidence.

They were both born and reared in the same city, Washington, D.C.

Both went to college in North Carolina, and though attending different universities, they lived in the same apartment house.

They both altered their career path dramatically after leaving school with each winding up working at the same restaurant on Hilton Head Island in South Carolina.

While both were on that island, they drove identical vehicles, and believe it or not, they were burgundy-colored Isuzu Troopers.

Despite such coincidence, commonality, and proximity, they had never met until one George applied for a position at the same Hilton Head restaurant where the other George was already employed.

George Spriggs and George Jackson have worked together ever since their first meeting in 1991, and they expect to maintain their relationship for a long time to come.

They now own and operate the North Beach Grill, an increasingly popular restaurant nestled unobtrusively between the Lighthouse Museum and the Shrine Club on Tybee's north end.

Restauranteurs George Spriggs, left, and George Jackson.

Their similarity, incidentally, does not extend to either their physical appearance or personality.

George Spriggs is a mountainous, rotund, gregarious man who spends a lot of time at the grill's counter regaling customers with colorful conversation and a ready laugh.

George Jackson is a tall, slim, strikingly handsome fellow who tends to be more than a trifle reserved, lingering in the background of the operation while handling most of the food purchases.

"I'll be in the back, doing whatever is necessary," he says. "I'm mostly the utility person."

Jackson has been married for 12 years, while Spriggs remains a bachelor.

Both commute here from their homes on Hilton Head but hope to move to Tybee soon.

Both Georges now participate in food preparation prior to their restaurant's opening each day, while Spriggs mostly handles the cooking to order once they open for business.

After completing high school in Washington, Spriggs, the son of a preacher, attended Duke University, majoring in comparative religions "mostly because I enjoyed it," he says.

"What I really planned to do at the time was become a doctor. I took all the science courses necessary and after I graduated, I worked for a year and then went to the University of North Carolina doing graduate work in chemistry."

"Then I woke up one morning and just said I don't want to do this. After all those years of planning (to be a doctor), it was just very clear. I didn't want to do it."

"Then it was a matter of finding out what I did want to do. I had notions of wanting to be a writer, so I moved to Hilton Head on Thanksgiving in 1987. I started working as a waiter and wound up working three jobs."

After starting a home health care service on Hilton Head, Spriggs soon found he was far too busy to pursue his dream of writing.

George Jackson was already on Hilton Head when Spriggs showed up but had followed a far more circuitous route to get there.

Jackson also left Washington when he completed high school, moving to Durham, N.C. where he attended N.C. Central College while renting an apartment in the same building where Spriggs lived.

After graduating he was employed in marketing with the Exxon Corp. for three years, then landed a job as a federal bank examiner.

"In '81, I had a complete career change," Jackson says. "I went into the hotel and food business. I started out with the Omni Hotel in Atlanta in food and beverage."

He remained with the Omni until 1984, then moved to the Ritz Carlton Hotel, working in the entertainment lounge when that hotel opened in Buckhead.

"It was a lot of fun," Jackson says. "It was THE place to be at the time. It was the only place to go in Buckhead."

Later, he was employed as restaurant manager with the Doubletree Hotel chain in Denver.

"They moved me up to their resort hotel in Vail, Colo.," he says. "That was a lot of fun. I learned to ski."

"Then I switched one resort town for another and moved to Hilton Head. I really needed to get back east to be nearer my family. There were some health problems, particularly with my mother."

Jackson was employed at the Hyatt Regency Hotel on Hilton Head before working at a couple of the upscale golf resorts on the island, and ultimately returning to restaurants.

"I'd go back and forth from managing places to actually waiting on tables and bartending," he says. "You can really make more money in those jobs and your hours are shorter."

One day, while walking near his house, he spotted

what he thought was his burgundy Isuzu Trooper.
George Spriggs was driving, and Jackson hurried
home trying to figure out "what that guy was doing
driving my car."

When he arrived, he was surprised to spot the car he
thought he had just seen still sitting in his driveway
right where he had parked it.

The two Georges finally got together a month or so
later, in 1991, when Spriggs applied for a job at the
Le Bistro restaurant.

Spriggs got the job and, although long overdue, finally met Jackson, who was working there, and they
quickly became friends after discovering they drove
identical cars.

It was Spriggs who found the site on Tybee through
a friend in Savannah who told him the lease on the
place had expired and he thought it might interest
George.

"It was a little shack that had been used as a hot dog
stand, but I saw what it could be," says Spriggs.

"I'd seen the full gamut of restaurants as a waiter. I
took the time to study each operation. I paid attention. I saw what worked and what didn't work. What
you could get away with based on where you were. I
thought this would work."

Enthusiastic, George hauled his friend George over to
see the place.

"I said, God, this is a mistake," says Jackson of his initial viewing.

"Don't look at it for what it is, look at it for what it can be," Jackson quotes Spriggs as saying.

Spriggs prevailed. They acquired the place in 1993 but were open only a couple of months that year and drew little business because dredging and sand replenishment work on the nearby beach kept beachgoers away.

Despite the original dearth of business, they remained convinced the restaurant had possibilities, and the lease was cheap.

"We knew if we wanted to draw people out here, we had to offer them something totally different, something they couldn't get any place else," says Jackson. Their basic concept was to serve all of the food fresh

View of the North Beach Grill when the two Georges acquired the property.

out of their own kitchen and, after careful consideration, agreed that a combination of Caribbean and Southern beach cuisine was what the island needed.

"Everybody had told me that this was the South and you had to give people here what they expected," says Spriggs. "We had to have food that goes along with the beach location. That meant crab and fish and shrimp. We blended the Southern and the Caribbean."

"The thing that put us on the map was our crab cakes. Like everything else here they're made from scratch. It's based on a recipe given to me by a former friend on Hilton Head. We spiced it up some. It's the spices and the combination of 'em that makes the difference."

"Our red beans and rice are probably the item which most people relate the Caribbean to. Plantain, not everybody likes 'em, but it's popular with those people who are looking for the islandy feel."

Another vital component, according to Spriggs, was selecting the right music for their restaurant.

"We wanted an eclectic kind of clientele, and we wanted something that everyone kind of relates to," he says.

Reggae was their ultimate choice since it worked with both the beach and the Caribbean fare.

They also started improving the little place. A full

kitchen was installed, and a deck outside was erected and covered with a large awning.

Another major move in their march toward success was the acquisition of a liquor license.

The following year business picked up and their lease was extended.

Business improved substantially with the summer season during which they concentrated on lunch, operating the restaurant from 11 AM until 7 in the evening.

A major break then occurred serendipitously when a customer asked them to serve dinner for a large group of his friends.

"We'd never planned on doing dinner, but we did it for him," says Spriggs.

That first dinner proved so successful that the Georges decided to make it a regular thing and now, except for the huge daytime crowds on summer Saturdays and Sundays, dinners have become their biggest business.

Jackson says the thing that really made the restaurant take off was the 1995 Bud Lite volleyball tournament which was staged in the parking lot beside their restaurant.

"That was a big plus for advertising and letting people know we were here," he says.

"We were getting tourists from the lighthouse and beach, but what we needed was to get people who lived within the county, and a lot of people knew we were here after that tournament. We did all the food for it."

He says they were not as disappointed as most people suspected when plans to stage the volleyball venue for the 1996 Olympics on the same site fell through.

"We kind of looked at it as a blessing in disguise," says Jackson. "There would have been a lot of changes and a lot of new structures needed for the facility."

"They would have had to have an Olympic volleyball court and a practice court and locker room facilities."

"I talked to the people planning the event and in all probability our restaurant would have been torn

The Grill shortly after the two Georges first acquired it.

down because of all the space they needed."

With or without the Olympics, business began to boom for the Georges with most of their customers coming from Savannah and Wilmington Island, rather than Tybee itself.

"Our reputation in town is pretty good," says Spriggs.

Their reputation has spread much further as well when the restaurant was written up in *Family Magazine* ("customers came in and told me about it, but I never saw the article," says Spriggs) and in *Gourmet* and *Glamour*.

"People go to the dentist's office and flip through the pages and see us," he says.

Flyers at the Visitors Center and hotels in Savannah have also lured customers, and tourists stumble upon the place when they visit the lighthouse and its museum, and Tybee's north end beach.

There are ten people working at the grill now during the peak season, seven of them on duty simultaneously.

They've even laid on a sous chef, Charlie Reeves, a gifted cabinetmaker widely known on the island for building beautiful wooden kayaks.

"He was a customer who came in here frequently and just sat there," says Spriggs. "We looked at each other all the time, but we never talked."

"Then one day he asked about a job. He'd had a lot of kitchen experience, and we decided to give him a try. He's from Cajun country and knew spices and that stuff, and it worked out well."

Spriggs laughs when he recalls first hearing the new sous chef's heavy Cajun accent.

"I just said don't talk to me. Talk to the other George. I can't understand a thing that you're saying. For the first couple of months, I kept asking what is he talking about?"

This is the first year the Georges have continued their operation during the winter. They're open Thursday through Sunday and doing a pretty good business, according to Spriggs.

They're now planning to expand the kitchen area and add another deck.

Based on their success on the island, they also have plans to open another restaurant in downtown Savannah.

Despite that initial language problem, their relationship with Reeves has worked out so well that they plan to name the proposed Savannah restaurant The Kayak Cafe in his honor.

If that venture proves successful, they want to open other restaurants in the area, likely based on the same theme as their Tybee grill.

"That was our intention all along," says Jackson.

"We always wanted to open more than one restaurant. We were thinking that after about the fourth year here we'd be ready. We're just about on track."

"Possibly, we'll even franchise the operation," says Spriggs. "We'll see how it goes."

The restaurant business is now in their blood and they couldn't be more pleased with their career change.

"We plan to stay with it," says Spriggs. "A one-time mom-and-pop operation was not what we were looking for. That wasn't our vision. This will probably get us to our early retirement."

Lunch crowd at the North Beach Grill.

Based on the strange coincidences that brought them together, fate does seem to be on their side, by George.

Sheldon Solomon -
A New Breed of Tybee Solomon

Beach Realtor
Eyes Development
In Thunderbolt

*T*ybee's Shell Solomon is spreading his already wide wings in real estate by heading to Thunderbolt.

Most folks think he's a Tybee "homey," given his familiar island name.

After all, the Solomons have proliferated on Tybee since around 1900.

It was A.P. Solomon II who operated the island's first waterworks.

His son, Edmund, now nearing 90, was Tybee's building and plumbing inspector from 1975 until 1991 and a founder of the Marine Rescue Squadron.

He still spends hours in the workshop back of his house carving birds and dolphins and creating a variety of other artsy-craftsy creations with his impressive collection of antique tools.

Edmund is the patriarch of the Solomon family, which now numbers several dozen on the island.

But Sheldon (Shell) Solomon is not one of them.

Despite his name and Tybee residency, Shell's what is known, usually affectionately hereabouts as a Damned Yankee.

Hey, who doesn't love Joe DiMaggio?

His mother, a Screven County native, met and married his father in Savannah during World War II, when his dad was stationed at Hunter Army Airfield.

Shell was born in Tampa, Fla., during his father's assignment there in 1944. After the war, the family returned to his dad's Chicago hometown, and that's where Shell grew up.

He is careful to note, however, that every summer his family made a ritual of returning to Savannah, and the beach at Tybee, for vacations.

His parents moved down permanently in the late 1970s, and Shell, who had migrated back to his birthplace in Tampa, headed to Atlanta to make his fortune about the same time.

He acquired a Dairy Queen franchise in the big city and, with a lot of help from his four young sons, built that business from a $90,000 gross in 1980 to a million-dollar annual volume seven years later.

On the list of individual Dairy Queen operations, Shell's soared from No. 5,250 when he bought it to No. 20 in the entire world during his ownership.

He says his sons were an enormous help in building the business, assisting with all aspects of the operation, from the cash register to making sundaes and sandwiches and making personnel decisions.

It may have been that experience which led one of his sons, Joel, to open his own restaurant, the now thriving Café Loco beside Lazaretto Creek, when the family moved to Tybee.

Shell had purchased a large house and several townhouses as investments and vacation escapes in 1984,

Shell Solomon discusses real estate ventures.

by which time his Dairy Queen had turned into a
cash cow.

After seven years in Atlanta, a man moseyed into
Shell's office and made him an offer to buy the business which he says he couldn't refuse.

"My business was not for sale, but his offer was just
too good to turn down," says Shell.

After shedding the business, Shell and his family set
out for Tybee, not with carpetbags but with a nice
little nest egg.

Shell figured he'd slow down and relax for a bit but
was not fixated on turning into a total beach bum.

"I had dabbled a bit in real estate and decided to
get my license, thinking it was something I like and
would be a lot less demanding than those 100-hour
weeks at the restaurant," he says.

Now he reckons restaurants and real estate have
many things in common, not the least of which are
hard work and long hours.

"And they both bring a lot of joy," he says. "When
you make a hot fudge sundae or a banana split, it's
fun when you see the customer break into a big grin.
It's like that when you sell a house for someone too.
You're making both people happy. Those people who
buy a house give you the best feeling because you've
found them a home."

Shortly after arriving on Tybee, domestic tranquility went haywire, and Shell wound up living in an apartment rather than the huge family home on Spanish Hammock. That house was sold when his marriage went south.

That slow-paced life he envisioned was speeded up perceptibly by the necessity of rebuilding his financial reserves following wedlock's demise.

Shell became a partner in the Tybee Island Realty Co. for a short time prior to establishing Solomon Properties, Inc. That company, with which well-known Tybee Realtor Bonnie Gaster was affiliated until recently, has likely sold more property than any other on the island.

Now Shell's invading the Savannah suburbs in a dramatic reversal of the normal process. Historically, it was Savannah entrepreneurs who headed to the beach to enhance their growing fortunes.

He just opened the first real estate office in Thunderbolt, where he expects sales to boom in connection with a posh new riverside condominium he's handling, along with other properties.

Shell opened his office on River Drive, just across the street from the site where the Thunderbolt Harbor Condominiums are under construction beside the Wilmington River.

His Thunderbolt Realty/Solomon Properties has exclusive sale rights for the new condominiums which will ultimately include 36 units ranging in price from $279,900 to $314,900.

Each of the 1,800 square foot condominiums will have a unique accouterment, according to Shell.

"This is the only waterfront residence in the area that you can get on the Intracoastal Waterway with your own boat slip," he says.

While the first brick has yet to be laid at the new complex, the enthusiastic realtor says he has already sold 10 units and is planning a marketing campaign to reach affluent boaters from as far away as Atlanta.

But Shell says the new condos are not the only reason he established his office in Thunderbolt.

"I go where opportunities lead and Thunderbolt is a great opportunity for sales," he says, noting that Thunderbolt is similar to what Tybee was when he started in real estate a decade ago and Savannah realtors have treated it like a stepchild for years.

"Waterfront is always popular and a prime area for sales, and Thunderbolt is right on the river and right next door to Savannah," he says, adding that he was amazed to learn that no permanent real estate office was located there.

Shell believes there are opportunities in Thunderbolt for resale of houses and condominiums which will continue into the future.

Shell stands beside the Wilmington River in Thunderbolt where new condos are being built.

"We've just established the office and are just looking into all the possibilities now," he said, while indicating he plans to initiate a marketing campaign for the entire area in the near future.

"I think there's an exceedingly strong opportunity here," he said. "Nobody has ever tried to come in here and do anything for these people. They treat Thunderbolt like they used to treat Tybee!"

While Shell operates two offices on Tybee, one on Tybrisa used principally to handle rental properties, and the other on Butler, this is the first branch office he has opened. It will be manned full time, with brokers alternating between that office and Tybee.

"That's the nice thing about this (Thunderbolt) operation," says Shell. "It's a small office with low overhead because it's a branch office, and I don't have to have a whole separate sales staff and broker.

"When my people are not busy at the Tybee office they can come down here, and we've put together schedules to rotate our people in and out, and it gives my people twice as many opportunities as walk-ins would."

Shell stands outside his new office in Thunderbolt.

Shell said he has received a lot of unexpected business from owners of two existing condominiums in Thunderbolt who want to resell their property. Those condos look out on the river but are situated across the road from it.

The Thunderbolt Harbor development is the only one directly beside the river. It is situated on pie-shaped property formerly occupied by a marina.

But building his business in Thunderbolt is only part of Shell's expansion plans.

Construction of a permanent office building for his real estate operations on Tybee's Butler Avenue, directly opposite the site of the old DeSoto Beach Hotel, is scheduled soon, with the site plan already having been approved.

Shell, who admits his familiar family name was a pretty good asset when he first started his operation on Tybee ("and even now neither side discourages the supposed connection when something good is being said about either family," he says), has developed a business that seems to be booming in every direction.

"I do my own thing and I try to take advantage of any opportunities that come along," he says. "I've bought and sold a lot of property over the years where there was a good opportunity."

He does not preclude the possibility of doing business in Savannah or pursuing sales in other, more distant areas.

"I've got a lot of time left to work and I more or less go where the opportunities lead," he says.

Meanwhile, Shell and his family have become deeply enmeshed in the fabric of Tybee through their industry and gregarious natures, and they're expanding in numbers.

"We've got seven in the immediate family now," says Shell of his clan.

Who knows? There may be an even larger Solomon Dynasty than those originals aborning.

POSTSCRIPT: That new building Shell Solomon planned on Butler Avenue never materialized. After his temporary offices on the site were destroyed by fire, he relocated his Tybee operation to a nearby location on First Street. Shell remarried and his new spouse subsequently acquired an expansive farm in Rincon, Georgia and now spend time between there and Tybee when they are not travelling extensively, although Shell says he continues to handle a bit of real estate business "because I just can't get away from that." Meanwhile, his son Joel shut down his restaurant on Lazaretto Creek and is following in his father's footsteps as a realtor with Solomon Properties. Joel says Shell's life of hard work and achievement, along with his being a great friend and father, continue to serve as a role model which he's hoping to emulate.

Freda Rutherford -
Your Choice: Advocate or Gadfly?

No Holds Barred
For This
Outspoken Islander

If civic or government action is needed on Tybee Island, you'll find her there, leading the charge.

Freda Rutherford may be the island's most active advocate for positive political change, or its archetypical political gadfly.

It's a coin toss on Tybee, where consensus is as alien as Cream o' Wheat for breakfast down South.

She weighs in vociferously on almost any hot issue with a voice that is not your typical steel magnolia, syrupy-sweet southern sound usually voiced by refined ladies hereabouts.

Hers comes at you in crisp, staccato bursts, mowing you down like a machinegun, a voice that meshes perfectly with her persona. It seems to scream for action... right now!

"Everybody thinks I'm a Yankee," she says. "They

really do, but I'm from the Ozarks. I learned to talk this way before I left the South. I figured if you didn't get it in fast, nobody'd listen to ya."

Freda is a dynamo on Tybee's Beach Task Force and Audit Committee, while also working with the Tybee Neighborhood Association, Lighthouse preservation efforts, and Tybee Fest, which was originally formed to help lure tourists to the island, especially during the winter off-season.

Freda Rutherford during campaign for city council.

She is omnipresent at city council meetings, where she addresses members on every issue imaginable.

Freda also serves as a font of information for residents through her computer, firing off e-mails about pertinent information she gleans from the news media and her extensive contacts on Tybee and in Savannah.

She promotes attendance at council sessions by sending out copies of its meeting agendas in advance, and many folks rely on her to inform them about other public meetings.

Members of her web network also use her site as a forum, responding to her and others about controversial issues such as the proposed widening of Highway 80.

"I've got a high energy level," she explains. "This is my town, you know, and I give opinions about things. Keeps my mind busy. I like trouble."

Despite her sometimes-curmudgeonly approach, Freda is optimistic about Tybee's future, and is particularly enthusiastic about the newly elected mayor and City Council taking office in January.

"I'm very happy with the election," she says. "I think there was a big message."

That message was reflected in the initial post-election city council meeting at which a 90-day moratorium on large condo construction was enacted, according to

Freda.

"With Shirley (Sessions) getting to be mayor pro tem and Dick Smith losing, they have a whole new attitude," she says.

Freda believes a strong bureaucracy would save council considerable trouble when it deals with important issues such as determining the proper building density on Tybee.

"What saves city hall's butt so much on Tybee is that you have so many volunteers that go in and do the work that staff should be able to do. You have (city councilman) Paul Wolff writing grants, God love him. There's something wrong with that picture."

Freda believes the new council will adopt different hiring practices, noting: "When I moved here, they said you couldn't get a job with the city. The only people who could get a job at city hall lived within two blocks of it, and it was pretty much true."

"It's too bad that it's assumed as employment of last resort for local yokels. I mean, that's not what government is, you know."

"I think we'll get it in hand. I'm really optimistic about that 'cause I don't think the new people that are coming in are going to tolerate it."

"They've got to build a professional staff. You're not a community of 3,500. You're a community of resources for 20,000 or something, and you gotta have that expertise, the planning expertise. It's just not there to get this community to be sophisticated enough to face the future on lots of complex issues."

One of the more surprising aspects of the recent election was that voter rolls showed 500 new voters have been added in the last two years, she says, and "the influx of people that you are seeing, strangely, are the ones who would like to see Tybee as it is, whereas the old timers, I think, are pretty taken up with the money, the opportunity to make money."

The impact of development on the infrastructure, particularly the availability of water, remains a major concern for Freda.

Freda stands behind Kathryn Williams, left, and Lisa Lepofsky during political planning session.

"They say we figure we've got enough water for 20 years," she says, then adds with a dubious frown, "Excuse me!"

Developers claim adding condo rental units poses no problem because the owners occupy them only a few months a year and use very little water, "but we expect when they retire, they're all going to move here. Well, if they do, your infrastructure really starts hurting."

Freda is also concerned about the future of the housing market.

Freda, left, and friend Shirley Wright, chairman of Forever Tybee, strike a happy pose.

"I think this housing market is going to crash and burn," she warns. "Then what happens? We could see these places all standing vacant. We could go down to the courthouse steps and buy some. Maybe that's what we do."

This has happened on Tybee previously, she says, pointing out that Racquet Club units sold for between $69,000 and $79,000 at 18% interest on mortgages in the 1980s, but by 1992 the same units were being sold "five for $100,000 at the courthouse."

Freda bought a Racquet Club condo for $33,000 when she moved to Tybee in 1993 and says a similar unit just sold "for $300,000, and that's what buyers are looking for, appreciation," because she sees no profit now in renting and claims that a small downturn in property values will be devastating.

Ethics in government is another of her concerns.

"We have a little problem now with the ethics ordinance," she says, referring to the current debate over whether to expand the committee's "duties to cover hearings or adopt a new ordinance and get a whole new audit committee."

Freda believes most violations are covered by the current ordinance and thinks the ethics ordinance debate "will shake out, but there is going to be a way that people can bring complaints, and council is going to have to hear them."

"They can't say no to any of this. Council members

have the ability to sanction each other now. Isn't that
cute?"

While Freda claims the Savannah Area Chamber of
Commerce fails to meet its contract obligations and
does nothing to help Tybee, she thinks the island
could enhance its revenue flow by planning and pro-
moting its tourist-attracting events year-round.

If the island produced a calendar of events, people
with money would come and "they would eat in our
restaurants and benefit our hotel and condo industry," she says.

"If you could ever pull that all together, that might
be the thing that could unite the community. Business owners might really believe that the government
and community don't hate them and have their best
interests at heart. That would keep our business
base."

"I want it to be a small town. I don't want it to be
all condos. I enjoy being able to go around the island
and go shopping and have all these things. I'm one of
those people who doesn't cross the bridge that much."

She does harbor some fear about the possibility that
a large hotel might be built on Tybee, or that the
height restriction, now set at 35 feet, could be raised,
although she thinks the height limit "may be the one
thing that is sacrosanct."

She says that if a previous push led by former Councilman Jimmy Burke to have water lines run from

Savannah to the island had been successful it would have opened Tybee up "for unlimited resources" which might have led to dropping this restriction and major development.

"If that doesn't happen, you're going to cap out on this stuff, but if the big money moves in, you get somebody like the Marriott who says they want to come here and buy out six or eight old beach houses and put something on the ocean, and they can throw lawyers at you 'til the cows come home."

Freda's move to the island from Michigan 12 years ago came as the result of her making a business trip to Savannah.

Left to right, Freda, Julia Pearce, Sandy McLeod and Shirley Sessions.

"I didn't know there was a Tybee, but I always wanted to live on the ocean," she says, referring to her discovery of the island while interviewing for a job with the City of Savannah.

"I liked what I saw," she says. The small-town atmosphere and friendliness are "delightful," and it was "like coming home" to the little community where she attended school as a child while living on her family's farm in the Ozarks.

Freda says one of the reasons she continues her activist role is because "I like to champion the underdog, particularly the poor people."

She did just that during her eight years' service as director of Workforce Development for Savannah, during which time her duties were expanded to include eight counties in the coastal area.

She also advocated for the underprivileged in her earlier career in Michigan, where she spearheaded programs for re-training and re-employment of laid-off workers.

Freda says there are major flaws in Savannah's school system.

"School boards are bad everywhere, but when you are in poor communities you sort of understand that" she says.

"Savannah is not a poor community. It has a high poverty factor, but it has incredible resources, and that's a different story."

"How Savannah can have the worst education system, you cannot explain to me. This is a cultured community with incredible wealth, incredible resources, which can't manage its schools."

"We ran summer youth programs" every year in Michigan putting about 1,500 children "to work in units of government and non-profits to teach them what work is. They had to be poor kids."

She found the situation was quite different when she started working in Savannah, however.

"Every year I would start in January trying to get a list from the schools," she says. "Some schools, like Bryan County, couldn't do enough for you because you were going to take their kids and pay them minimum wage to work in the summertime."

"In Chatham County you couldn't get the list out of them."

The local power structure, including the business community, offers little more than lip service to underprivileged school children, many of whom are not even informed about job placement programs for high school graduates, according to Freda, who says the absence of a support system for poor children who get in trouble is coming back to haunt the community.

Freda on beach at annual Polar Bear Swim.

"Kids make a lot of mistakes," she says. "When they've got parents standing behind them with the wherewithal to do something about it, you don't hear about it."

"I raised three of them. How many times did I prop their little butts up, and get them out of scrapes, and send them back to school?"

"Middle class kids do that. But when they're poor kids, these kids out there creating all this crime, they don't have anybody to come to straighten them out, put them back on the right track, four, five, six times, however many times parents do those kinds of things."

"If you don't help the underprivileged, you create an underclass who has no hope, no resources" and you become a good target because "you probably have a wallet in your back pocket, and that's what you've left yourself open for."

"It's like living in a Third World country where you're unsafe on the streets. Do you really want to live like that? It's in your own best interest. That's why you bother with them."

Based on her own experience, Freda disavows the theory that "people are poor because they are bad. Luck has a lot to do with it. Luck sure had a lot do with my life."

Freda, who married at 17 and had three children by the time she was 20, received her beautician's license before she finished high school in Detroit, where she and her mother operated three beauty salons at one time.

"I got tired of standing on my feet and putting up

with rich women by the time I was 30," she says. "It wasn't something I wanted to do the rest of my life, so I went back to college, got my undergraduate degree, and studied for my master's at the University of Michigan."

Armed with this education, she landed a job as employment director of the Downriver Community Conference Re-Employment Program, covering 17 communities, primarily running public service employment programs helping "disadvantaged folks to get in school."

That area, just south of Detroit, became snarled in a recession in the early 1980s, resulting in massive lay-offs and hard times.

A multi-national chemical company in one of her towns shut down, and the mayor asked for assistance.

"Jimmy Carter was running hard for re-election, and he had a 10-point plan, one of them about re-employment," she recalls.

"We wrote a grant request to the labor secretary. They were looking for something fast, and all of a sudden, we were on the front page of every newspaper in the country and around the world!"

Those were pretty heady times for Freda, who says she was called to testify before Dan Quayle's Senate Employment Productivity Committee "before anybody knew who Dan Quayle was."

That experience was more than a little traumatic, she says, noting: "They sit you in a pit and they turn the lights on you. It was like an inquisition. After that, there's nothing that can intimidate you."

Freda's group was successful in obtaining a $4 million line item to help those who lost their jobs in Michigan plant closings.

Freda happily sorts items for Forever Tybee yard sale.

The item was so small that "(David) Stockman never bothered to look at it," but, while remaining in subsequent budgets "it took us 18 months to convince them funding the program was a good idea," she says.

"Then we became the darlings of the Republicans. When Reagan finally decided this was a good idea, we put up six pilot programs," where only one existed under Carter.

Freda helped design and launch those programs. About a year later she was recruited by General Motors to "work for a vice president of the UAW and a vice president of General Motors for 18 months, and you can't beat that. Talk about being the jelly in the sandwich!"

Freda opened a re-employment center for GM and the UAW in downtown Detroit before taking a position running employment programs for Wayne County, serving 42 communities just outside Detroit.

She says she spent a lot of time in meetings, awaiting approval for various projects and "it was pretty boring."

But she was far from bored when she traveled to Pittsburgh to participate in the Regional/Urban Development Assistance Team (RE/UDAT) program, an annual volunteer project of the American Institute of Architecture.

The team's goal was to redesign small, economically depressed mill towns, and they wanted Freda "to talk about the people who had been laid off."

She spent a week with the architects, including four representatives of Britain's Royal Institute of Architecture, among them the architect for Prince Charles, touring mill towns, then preparing comprehensive reports for town meetings.

During the frenzied work week, it was announced that Prince Charles would attend the annual AIA conference the following Sunday, and Freda, the only female and only non-architect present, was asked to be the spokesperson for RE/UDAT, greet the prince, and introduce him to the group.

After she agreed, she was told she would have to curtsy when she met Prince Charles since "a woman can't shake hands with the prince, and here's this guy showing me how to do this thing."

Freda, center, flanked by Dickie Trotter, left, and Lisa Lepofsky, right, pose to illustrate speak, hear and see no evil.

"I stood my ground and said I ain't gonna curtsy! Arrogant through and through, don't do no curtsy."

"So, that's my job, to say Hi prince, here's where we're at, and hand him off to the first design team, and they pass him around. I figure I've got 30 seconds. I can do this."

"So, he comes down the line, sees me and says 'I'm so happy to be here. I just have to tell you, while I'm in New York, my tire blew out,' and Gee Whiz! He's wanting to hold a conversation, and I ain't gonna have no conversation with no prince. I gotta get through this!"

Just as Freda passed Prince Charles along, a man standing behind her leaned over and said: "That's OK, Chuck, don't let it happen again."

"I'm throwing my hands up in the air laughing" when a photographer took the picture which appeared in the Pittsburgh papers the next day. That's the day I met the prince. It was a nice moment."

Freda was a member of the National Association of Counties Employment Committee in 1984, when the group held its annual conference in Savannah, "and I loved it," she says.

Nine years later, an associate who knew how much she liked the city, informed her about the director's job opening in Savannah, and she applied.

Freda is particularly pleased to be able to pursue her
interest in improving the island as an independent
citizen.

"One of the things I like about Tybee work is they
can't do anything about me," she says. 'When you
work for the government, you've always got political
considerations. You've always got constraints. You've
always got the people you've got to be nice to."

With no such restraints on the island, Freda is doing things her way here. Like it or not, you'll always
know exactly where she stands.

**POSTSCRIPT: _Freda has departed the seashore
for the mountains, moving to Brevard, NC. Rest
assured, however, that she still stays in touch
with the island's happenings, especially its politics, through frequent phone calls to her activist
friends on Tybee._**

Appendix

The articles in this volume were originally published in the Savannah Morning News. The original publication dates for each are as follows:

Acknowledgements

Like most writers, I am indebted to a number of people who contributed substantially to bringing this book to fruition.

I want to give a special thanks to my dear sister, Jackie Eggerton, for her excellent and expeditious proofreading of each of the chapters in this book, along with her always loving support and helpful advice.

I also want to thank Suzi Fuchs, a former print journalist and friend for more years than either of us is anxious to acknowledge, for her inciteful suggestions and editing of a number of my columns early on in this effort.

I am grateful to Tybee Island newspaper columnist and author Ben Goggins for his helpful editing, advice, and kind words of encouragement.

Miranda Carter was especially helpful in re-typing old columns which were not preserved in my computer files, while Tybee environmentalist, author, calligrapher, and artist Mallory Pearce did outstanding work creating the caricatures of the subjects of each chapter.

Layout Designer Lauren Clackum, known hereabouts fondly as the "Princess of Pages," did all the formatting and layout for the book in a timely and professional manner which made her extraordinary craftsmanship seem deceptively effortless.

My special thanks also goes out to the families and/or friends of the subjects in this book who provided photographs which were not available in my files. These included photos of Benjamin Alexander in chapter one, Richard and Mary Grosse in chapter two, Bill Inglis in chapter seven, Edmund Solomon in chapter ten, Rick and Debbie Sheridan in chapter fourteen, Peter Bannon in chapter twenty, George Spriggs and George Jackson in chapter twenty two, and Freda Rutherford in chapter twenty four.

I am also grateful to all those who encouraged me to continue with this project along the way.

Without each of you this book would likely never have seen the light of day.

About the Author

Born in Atlanta, GA., J. R. Roseberry has resided in the Far East and the eastern U.S. from Florida to New York, with stops in Georgia, South Carolina, Virginia, Tennessee, and Maryland in between.

After living in Atlanta, Knoxville, TN., Anderson and Columbia, SC, as a child, he attended high schools in Pensacola, FL, Rochester, NY, Norfolk, VA, and Leonardtown and St. Mary's City, MD.

Receiving his driver's license at 13, he purchased his first car at 16, the same age at which he became the youngest Red Cross Certified Water Safety Instructor in Maryland and taught swimming classes for dozens of children while also conducting Senior Life Saving courses for college students.

During his senior year in high school he was employed as the Beach Concession Manager, bartender and night cashier at the U.S. Naval Air Station Officer's Club in Patuxent River, MD.

While earning a journalism degree at the University of South Carolina, he won a position as the youngest summer intern at the Atlanta Journal, then was hired as a full-time staff reporter for The State, South Carolina's largest newspaper, where he was employed throughout his junior and senior years.

Immediately after graduating in 1957, he moved to Tokyo, Japan where he pursued graduate studies at Sophia University while employed as a reporter and Photo Editor for Pacific Stars & Stripes, before moving to Okinawa, as an editor for the Okinawa Morning Star and Ryukyus representative for the Associated Press. While employed at the Star, he also designed and served as editor of the paper's monthly entertainment magazine.

Returning to the U.S. in 1961, J.R. became city hall reporter and later Sunday Magazine editor for the Savannah Morning News in Savannah, GA.

He was then hired by the Norfolk Virginian-Pilot, remaining in Norfolk, VA, for five years as reporter and ultimately Night City Editor before joining the staff of the Washington Post in the nation's capital.

While at the Post, he served as late night city editor directing coverage of the riots following the assassination of Martin Luther King Jr., before working with Bob Woodward and Carl Bernstein during their Watergate coverage.

J.R. joined a group of key editors in creating the Style section, which featured entertainment, society, and feature stories by nationally known writers. That section was the first on any major newspaper to replace traditional women's pages and it proved so successful that it was emulated by every large newspaper in the country.

He then moved to the news desk as Metropolitan News

Editor and joined a team of editors working with IBM in one of initial efforts to incorporate computers in newspaper operations.

After being given the newspaper's newly created title of Production Editor, he re-designed the newspaper, from its former narrow nine columns per page to six columns.

Later, he was named Pre-press Production Manager in which capacity he played a key role in converting the newspaper's production from the historic hot metal process to cold type and offset printing.

When the company purchased The Washington Star, which had previously been the country's preeminent afternoon newspaper, J. R. was placed in charge of the Star's facilities where he managed its medical office, restaurant, railroad siding for delivery of newsprint, mailroom, security staff and pressroom.

Under his leadership the plant became the principal printing facility for the Washington Post and won an award for having the best newspaper reproduction quality of any newspaper in the entire country utilizing the Napp printing process.

J.R. retired in 1992 after more than 20 years' with the Post, then travelled to Tybee Island where he returned to his journalistic roots writing a weekly column called "J.R.'s Island View" for the Savannah Morning News. The column consisted primarily of interviews with colorful characters on Tybee and the surrounding islands with a view toward preserving their histories while they were still able to share them.

In the late 1990s, he purchased and published The Tybee News newspaper, through which he was able to
shine a light on government actions and events on the
island which was receiving little coverage by any other
news media.

After incorporating the use of color and substantially
increasing the newspaper's size and circulation, he sold
it around the turn of the century and started freelance
writing for area and national publications while also
trying his hand at writing both fiction and music.

His winning short story in a competition for writers
throughout the southeastern U.S. was published in the
Savannah Anthology, while area musicians performed
and recorded his songs.

During the Covid 19 pandemic friends urged J.R. to
publish a compilation of his newspaper columns in a
book featuring islanders who helped make Tybee the
Mecca for tourists and retirees it is today.

You are now reading the third book in a series which is
the result of those suggestions.